v072610
pc: 254
isbn: 1932733388

Adobe Captivate 5:
The Essentials

"Skills and Drills" Learning

Kevin A. Siegel

iCONLOGiC
"Skills and Drills" Learning

Contents

About This Book
About the Author.. vii
About IconLogic Books vii
Book Conventions.. viii
Confidence Check viii
System Requirements viii
Data Files... ix
    Download the PC Data Files ix
    Download the Mac Data Files x
Need More Books?.. xi

Module 1: eLearning and Captivate
Education Through Pictures... 2
Planning eLearning Projects 4
The Captivate Interface 7
    Explore a Project 7
Workspaces 9
    Explore the Default Workspaces 9
    Modify and Reset a Workspace... 11
    Create a Workspace 13
    Navigate a Project... 15
Previewing 16
    Preview a Project 16
    Zoom Closer to a Slide... 18

Module 2: Recording Demos and Sims
Resolution and Recording Size.. 20
The Development Process 21
Preparing to Record 23
    Rehearse a Script 24
    Edit Recording Settings 25
    Set Recording Keys 27
Access for Assistive Devices 28
    Enable Access for Assistive Devices 28
Demonstrations... 29
    Record a Demonstration.. 29
Assessment Simulations 34
    Record an Assessment 34
Training Simulations 37
    Record a Training Simulation 37
Custom Recordings.. 40
    Record a Custom Simulation 41

Module 3: Captions, Styles and Timing
Text Captions 46
    Duplicate a Slide and Hide the Mouse.................................. 46
    Insert, Resize and Move Text Captions 48
    Modify Text Caption Properties... 51
Caption Styles 55
    Edit the Default Caption Style 55
    Reset an Object Style 57
    Change an Object's Position & Size 58
The Timeline... 59
    View the Timeline.. 59
    Change a Slide's Display Time.. 60
    Use the Timeline to Set Object Display Times........................ 61

Show/Hide Timeline Objects 62
Use the Properties Panel to Control Timing 63
Set Mouse Properties 66
Check Spelling 67
Align Slide Objects 69

Module 4: Images and Drawing Objects
Slide Quality 74
Change Slide Background Quality 74
Blank Slides 75
Insert and Delete Slides 75
Images 76
Insert an Image 76
Set Image Size and Slide Position 78
The Library 79
Use the Library 79
Manage Unused Project Assets 82
Image Editing 83
Crop an Image 83
Create an Image Watermark 85
Control Image Timing and Transition 86
Work With Image Stacks 88
Mouse Visuals and Sounds 90
Add a Visual Click and Sound 90
Drawing Objects 92
Draw a Line 92

Module 5: Pointers, Buttons and Highlight Boxes
Pointer Paths and Types 96
Modify the Mouse Pointer 96
Buttons 98
Edit Slide and Object Display Times 98
Insert a Text Button 99
Set a Button's Timing and Options 101
Work With Image Buttons 102
Highlight Boxes 104
Insert and Format a Highlight Box 104

Module 6: Rollovers and Zoom Areas
Rollover Captions 110
Insert a Rollover Caption 110
Rollover Images 114
Insert a Rollover Image 114
Zoom Areas 116
Insert a Zoom Area 116
Rollover Slidelets 118
Insert and Format a Rollover Slidelet 118
Format the Slidelet 120
Add a Caption and Image to a Slidelet 121

Module 7: Audio
Importing Audio Files 124
Add Audio to a Slide Object 124
Add Background Audio 126
Slide Notes 127
Add a Slide Note 127

Recording Audio 128
    Calibrate a Microphone 128
    Record a Narration 130
    Import Voice Narrations 132
    Edit an Audio File 133
Silence 135
    Insert Silence 135
Text-to-Speech 137
    Convert Text-to-Speech 137

Module 8: Flash Video, Animation and Effects
Flash Video 140
    Insert Flash Video 140
    Set Flash Video Properties 141
Animation 144
    Add Animation to a Slide 144
Text Animation 146
    Insert Text Animation 146
Object Effects 148
    Apply a Fly-In Effect to a Text Caption 148
    Apply a ZigZag Motion Path 149

Module 9: Click and Text Entry Boxes
Demonstrations versus Simulations 152
    Hide the Mouse 152
Find and Replace 153
    Replace Phrases 153
Click Boxes 155
    Insert a Click Box 155
Text Entry Boxes 159
    Insert a Text Entry Box 159

Module 10: Introduction to Question Slides
Quiz Setup 164
    Edit Quizzing Object Styles 164
    Set the Quiz Preferences 165
Add Question Slides 168
    Insert Question Slides 168
    Format a Question Slide 169
    Add an Image to a Question Slide 171
    Paste as Background 172

Module 11: Publishing
URL Actions 176
    Link to a Web Site 176
Skins 179
    Apply a Skin 179
    Edit and Save a Skin 180
    Delete a Skin 181
Table of Contents 183
    Create a TOC 183
Preloaders 185
    Add a Loading Screen 185
Publishing 187
    Publish a Flash (SWF) 187
    Publish Word Handouts 190

Round Tripping 192
    Export Captions 192
    Perform a "Round Trip" 194
Want to Learn More About Adobe Captivate? 195

Appendix: FMRs, Panning, Manual Mode & Slideshows
Full Motion Recording 198
    Create an FMR 198
Panning 202
    Record a Lesson With Panning 202
Manual Mode 206
    Record Manually 206
Image Slideshows 208
    Create an Image Slideshow 208

iCONLOGiC

"Skills and Drills" Learning

About This Book

About the Author

Kevin Siegel is the founder and president of IconLogic, Inc. He has written more than 100 step-by-step computer training books, including *Essentials of Adobe Captivate 4, Adobe Captivate 4: Beyond the Essentials, Essentials of Adobe Captivate 3, Essentials of Adobe Captivate 2, Essentials of Macromedia Captivate, Essentials of RoboDemo 5, Essentials of Adobe RoboHelp 8, Essentials of Adobe RoboHelp 7, Essentials of Adobe Dreamweaver CS3, QuarkXPress 8: The Basics, Essentials of Adobe InDesign CS3, Camtasia Studio 7: The Essentials* and *Camtasia Studio 6: The Essentials*.

Kevin spent five years in the U.S. Coast Guard as an award-winning photojournalist and has more than two decades experience as a print publisher, technical writer, instructional designer and eLearning developer. He is a certified technical trainer, has been a classroom instructor for more than 18 years and is a frequent speaker at trade shows and conventions. Kevin holds multiple certifications from companies such as Adobe and the CompTIA. You can reach Kevin at **ksiegel@iconlogic.com**.

About IconLogic Books

IconLogic books are unique! They are created by instructors with years of software training experience. Before IconLogic books, our instructors rarely found a book that was perfect for a classroom setting. If the book was beautiful, odds were that the text was too small to read and hard to follow. If the text in a book was the right size, the quality of exercises left something to be desired.

Finally tiring of using inadequate materials, our instructors started teaching without any books at all. Over the years, we've had many students ask if the in-class instruction came from a book. If so, they said they'd buy the book. That sparked an idea. We asked students—just like you—what they wanted in a training manual. You responded and the results appear in this book.

We hope you enjoy the book. If you have any comments or questions, please see page xi for our contact information.

Book Conventions

This book has been divided into several modules. Since each module builds on lessons learned in a previous module, we recommend that you complete each module in succession. During every module, you will be guided through lessons step by step. Instructions for you to follow will look like this:

❑ instructions for you to follow will look like this

If you are expected to type anything or if something is important, it will be set in bold type like this:

❑ type **9** in the box

When asked to press a key on your keyboard, the instruction will look like this:

❑ press [**shift**]

Confidence Check

You will also come across the little guy at the right. He indicates a Confidence Check. Throughout each module you will be guided through hands-on exercises. But at some point you'll have to fend for yourself. That is where Confidence Checks come in. They're very important. You must be sure to complete each of them because some exercises build on completed Confidence Checks.

System Requirements

The Adobe Captivate 5 software does not come with this book. The software can be purchased directly from Adobe (**http://www.adobe.com**). You can also download a trial version of Captivate from Adobe. There are no limitations on the trial and it will last for 30 days from the day you install it on your computer. Here are Adobe's system requirements for installing and using Captivate 5.

Windows: Adobe Captivate 5, 1GHz or faster processor, Intel Pentium 4, Intel Centrino, Intel Xeon, or Intel Core Duo (or compatible) processor, Microsoft Windows XP with Service Pack 2 (Service Pack 3 recommended); Windows Vista Home Premium, Business, Ultimate, or Enterprise with Service Pack 1; or Windows 7, 1GB minimum RAM (2GB recommended), 3GB of available hard-disk space for installation; additional free space required during installation (cannot install on flash-based storage devices), DVD-ROM drive, 1,024x576 display (1,280x1024 is recommended) with 16-bit video card, Broadband Internet connection required for online services.

Mac: Adobe Captivate 5, Multicore Intel processor, Mac OS X v10.5.7 or v10.6, 1GB minimum RAM (2GB recommended), 3GB of available hard-disk space for installation; additional free space required during installation (cannot install on a volume that uses a case-sensitive file system or on flash-based storage devices), DVD-ROM drive, 1,024x576 display (1,280x1024 is recommended) with 16-bit video card, Broadband Internet connection required for online services.

You will also need Microsoft Word 2000 or newer on your computer. Word is used during the exporting activities beginning on page 190. If Word is not installed, you will not be able to complete all of the activities.

Data Files

The data files that support the lessons presented in this book can be downloaded from the IconLogic Web site. If you are using a PC, complete the activity below. Mac users, complete the activity on the next page.

Student Activity: Download the PC Data Files

1. Download the student data files necessary to complete the lessons presented in this book.

   ❒ start a Web browser
   ❒ go to the following Web address: **http://www.iconlogic.com/pc.htm**
   ❒ click the **Captivate 5: The Essentials** link

   Note: If the address above isn't working or is running slowly, the data files for this book (it's an EXE) can also be downloaded from **http://files.me.com/ iconlogic/nwmc5u**, which is our backup data files server.

   On most browsers, a dialog box will appear asking if you want to Save, Run or Open the file.

   ❒ click the **Save** button and save the file to your desktop

2. After the file downloads, close the Web browser.

3. Extract the data files.

   ❒ find the **Captivate5EssentialsData** file you just downloaded to your desktop
   ❒ double-click the file to open it (it's an EXE file containing the zipped data files)
   ❒ confirm **C:** appears in the **Unzip to Folder** area
   ❒ click the **Unzip** button
   ❒ click the **OK** button
   ❒ click the **Close** button after the files have been extracted to your hard drive

   The data files you will need for this book have now been installed to your hard drive (within a folder named **Captivate5EssentialsData**). As you move through the lessons in this book, you will be working with these files.

   The next activity is only for Mac users.

Student Activity: Download the Mac Data Files

1. Download the student data files necessary to complete the lessons presented in this book.

   ☐ start **Safari**

   ☐ go to the following Web address: **http://www.iconlogic.com/mac.htm**

   ☐ click the **Captivate 5: The Essentials** link

   The zipped data files will be downloaded to your **Downloads** folder and automatically extracted into a folder.

   Note: If the address above isn't working or is running slowly, the data files for this book (a zip file) can also be downloaded from **http://files.me.com/ iconlogic/4vfs5m**, which is our backup data files server.

2. Move the data files folder to your desktop.

   ☐ drag the **Captivate5EssentialsData** folder from the **Downloads** folder to your desktop

3. You can now close the **Downloads** folder and the Web browser.

Need More Books?

We are proud to offer books on the following subjects:

Editing and Grammar

Abrams' Guide to Grammar: Second Edition

Editing With MS Word 2007

eLearning

Captivate versions 3 thru 5

Camtasia Studio versions 6 thru 7

Help Authoring

Adobe RoboHelp HTML 6 thru 8

Print Publishing (Page Layout)

InDesign CS2 thru CS3

QuarkXPress versions 6 thru 8

Web Page Design and Development

Dreamweaver versions MX 2004 thru CS3

and there are more coming all the time.

Contact Information and Ordering

IconLogic, Inc.
3320 Breckenridge Way | Riva, MD 21140 | 410.956.4949
Web: **www.iconlogic.com** | E-mail: **orders@iconlogic.com**

iCONLOGiC

"Skills and Drills" Learning

Rank Your
Skills

Before starting this book, complete the skills assessment on
the next page.

iCONLOGiC
Adobe Captivate 5 Skills Assessment

How This Assessment Works

Below you will find 10 course objectives for *Adobe Captivate 5: The Essentials*. **Before starting the book:** Review each objective and rank your skills using the scale next to each objective. A rank of ① means **No Confidence** in the skill. A rank of ⑤ means **Total Confidence**. After you've completed this assessment, go through the entire book. **After finishing the book:** Review each objective and rank your skills now that you've completed the book. Most people see dramatic improvements in the second assessment after completing the lessons in this book.

Before-Class Skills Assessment

1. I can record a Custom project.   ① ② ③ ④ ⑤
2. I can create a Rollover Slidelet.   ① ② ③ ④ ⑤
3. I can insert a Text Caption.   ① ② ③ ④ ⑤
4. I can add Click Boxes.   ① ② ③ ④ ⑤
5. I can insert Highlight Boxes.   ① ② ③ ④ ⑤
6. I can insert Rollover Captions.   ① ② ③ ④ ⑤
7. I can add Text Entry Boxes.   ① ② ③ ④ ⑤
8. I can create a TOC using the Skin Editor. ① ② ③ ④ ⑤
9. I can perform a "round-trip" to Word.   ① ② ③ ④ ⑤
10. I can publish a SWF.   ① ② ③ ④ ⑤

After-Class Skills Assessment

1. I can record a Custom project.   ① ② ③ ④ ⑤
2. I can create a Rollover Slidelet.   ① ② ③ ④ ⑤
3. I can insert a Text Caption.   ① ② ③ ④ ⑤
4. I can add Click Boxes.   ① ② ③ ④ ⑤
5. I can insert Highlight Boxes.   ① ② ③ ④ ⑤
6. I can insert Rollover Captions.   ① ② ③ ④ ⑤
7. I can add Text Entry Boxes.   ① ② ③ ④ ⑤
8. I can create a TOC using the Skin Editor. ① ② ③ ④ ⑤
9. I can perform a "round-trip" to Word.   ① ② ③ ④ ⑤
10. I can publish a SWF.   ① ② ③ ④ ⑤

IconLogic, Inc.
3320 Breckenridge Way, Riva, MD 21140
www.iconlogic.com

iCONLOGiC

"Skills and Drills" Learning

Module 1: eLearning and Captivate

In This Module You Will Learn About:

- Education Through Pictures, page 2
- Planning eLearning Projects, page 4
- The Captivate Interface, page 7
- Workspaces, page 9
- Previewing, page 16

And You Will Learn To:

- Explore a Project, page 7
- Explore the Default Workspaces, page 9
- Modify and Reset a Workspace, page 11
- Create a Workspace, page 13
- Navigate a Project, page 15
- Preview a Project, page 16
- Zoom Closer to a Slide, page 18

Education Through Pictures

In a previous life, I was a professional photographer. When I wasn't snapping photos during an exhilarating stint with the U.S. Coast Guard in the early 1980s, I covered media events in New York City. To make extra money (as with all branches of the military, the Coast Guard didn't pay very well), I even covered a wedding or two. (I should point out that it was one wedding in particular that convinced me to plot a different career path besides photography once my Coast Guard tour was done... but that is another story.)

As any photographer can tell you, a primary goal is to capture a story with a few, or maybe just one, photograph. I'm betting that you have heard the phrase "A picture is worth a thousand words" at least a few times. As a photographer, I lived those words.

During my career, I have had the fortune of adding instructional designer, technical writer and technical trainer to my communications arsenal. And I have spent the bulk of my career attempting to perfect the art of teaching often complicated software applications to busy (and often distracted) adult learners as efficiently as possible. I have always attempted to write documentation using as few words as possible.

If you are in the business of educating, you know how difficult the job of writing relevant lesson plans with fewer words can be. My step-by-step books have long been known for their skills-and-drills approach to learning.

The term "skills-and-drills" learning means different things to different people. For some, it means fast-moving lessons that do not drown a person with unnecessary information. For me, "skills-and-drills learning" means learning—with pictures instead of words.

I learned long ago that humans, as a species, think not with words, but with pictures. Not sure what I'm talking about? Here's an example: Please close your eyes for a second and picture *three* in your mind's eye. (Open your eyes after a few seconds and move to the next paragraph—see how precise I was... I just know that some of you are gonna fall fast asleep without that last instruction.)

I wasn't specific when I asked you to picture *three* was I? It's a good bet that things such as *three cupcakes*, *three bowls of ice cream* or *three big boxes of Cap'n Crunch* (everyone knows that that's the best breakfast cereal *ever*) flashed into your mind's eye. Maybe a large numeral 3 appeared in your mind's eye—not the word "three," but a picture of a 3. The point is, I doubt that you visualized the word *three*. Why? Most of us think in terms of pictures, not words. For this reason, my books often contain hundreds of screen captures that quickly explain, with more pictures and fewer words, a concept that could take many paragraphs to describe.

RoboDemo to Captivate

A picture can be nice, but it's static. No matter how good a picture is, it can never tell specific information or show a concept in detail. For that reason, I went in search of a program I could use to augment the lessons taught in my books. Over the years I found several programs that I liked. The programs captured my computer's screen and mouse actions well enough, but the resulting lessons were *huge*. A five-minute eLearning lesson could easily gobble up nearly 100 mb of storage space on my Web server. Downloading a file that large over the Internet would take a lot of time, even with a fast Internet connection. Large file sizes were just part of the problem. The projects were not cross-platform (they would not work on both Macs and PCs) and there was not much interactivity, if any. You'll learn the value of adding interactivity to your eLearning lessons beginning on page 151.

The technology for creating interactive lessons was so bad that I decided to give up on the concept and wait until someone came up with a program that had what it takes to be a useful tool. That program arrived around 2002 and was known as Flashcam (by Nexus Concepts 2002). Flashcam, which was pretty much just a screen capture utility, became the property of eHelp Software (of current Adobe RoboHelp fame). eHelp Software, which renamed Flashcam as *RoboDemo*, was purchased by Macromedia (of Dreamweaver and Flash fame). Macromedia revamped RoboDemo, added some much-needed features and changed the name to *Captivate*. In 2005, Adobe acquired Macromedia. Hence, the program has been known as *Adobe Captivate*.

Using Captivate, you can create eLearning projects from anything you can access from your computer. The lessons you create can be interactive—you can add captions, rollovers, clickable areas, typing areas and sound effects.

Captivate projects can be exported to Small Web Format (SWF), executable files, Word documents, PDFs and AVIs. The published SWFs will be cross-platform, meaning that they can be viewed via a Web browser (such as Internet Explorer or FireFox).

> **Note:** You might find yourself in a debate as to what the SWF suffix stands for (you may have noticed above that I used the words "Small Web Format" to define a SWF). Admittedly, I originally thought SWF stood for "Shockwave File." In reality, the suffix once stood for "Shockwave Flash." The name was often confused with Macromedia's Shockwave format used for a program called Macromedia Director (that program lives today as Adobe Director). To end the confusion, Macromedia decided that SWF would forevermore stand for "Small Web Format."

Planning eLearning Projects

By the time you finish the last lesson in this book, you *will* be able to use Captivate to create eLearning lessons. The projects you learn to create will work the way Captivate's designers intended. However, just because you will soon be able to create technically solid Captivate projects does not necessarily mean you will go out and create good projects. If you want to create good, useful projects you have to plan ahead. Before recording your first real project, you should ask yourself the following questions:

❑ Who is my audience?

❑ What do I want my lessons to teach my audience?

❑ Is my audience young or old?

❑ Is my audience educated?

❑ Is my audience hearing challenged?

❑ Do I want my projects to contain images and background music? If so, where will I get them?

❑ Will there be captions (written instructions and descriptions)? If so, who will write the captions?

❑ Will I use a storyboard or script? (**Storyboards** are rough sketches that show the general content of your project, slide by slide. If your projects contain more screen shots of an application than captions, a storyboard is a good idea. **Scripts**, which are detailed step-by-step procedures, are ideal if your project will contain a significant number of captions.)

❑ Do I want my projects to be demonstrations, assessments or a combination of both?

When planning projects, keep in mind that the most useful projects contain the following basic elements:

❑ Title slide (telling the audience what they are going to learn)

❑ Credits and Copyright slide

❑ Narration, music and other sound effects

❑ Images and animations

❑ Interactivity (click boxes, text entry boxes and buttons)

❑ An ending slide (reviewing what the audience learned)

Budgeting Considerations

Many new Captivate developers underestimate development time needed to produce projects. The following table should help.

Project Size	Number of Development Hours
Small Projects (1-25 slides)	1-4 hours of production
Medium Projects (26-75 slides)	4-7 hours of production
Large Projects (80-150 slides)	8-10 hours of production
Bloated Projects (more than 150 slides)	Consider splitting projects this large into smaller projects.

I bet you're wondering what "production" means, especially considering the fact that most of the projects you create will likely be in the large category (80-150 slides) and take you, on average, 10 hours to produce.

Production Does Not Include

To begin, let's consider what "production" does **not** include. As mentioned on page 4, you'll need a script and/or storyboard.

❑ Storyboards: Rough sketches that show the general content of your project, slide by slide. If your projects contain more screen shots of an application than captions, a storyboard is a good idea.

❑ Scripts: Detailed step-by-step procedures. These are ideal if your project will contain a significant number of captions.

A typical one-hour eLearning course consists of 12, five-minute lessons. It could take up to three hours to write each of those lessons. Therefore, you should budget 40 hours to write the entire one-hour eLearning course. Depending on how fast you write, you could easily double those hours, meaning you may need to budget 80 hours for writing... which has nothing at all to do with Captivate production.

Production won't include creating a Captivate template, a completed shell project that you will use as the basis of all of your projects. It's not difficult to create a template, but it will take time. An ideal template will contain placeholders, an introduction slide, transitional slides, a conclusion slide, a skin and appropriate Start and End Properties (while these terms may seem foreign to you now, you will learn about many of them as you move through lessons presented in this book).

Finally, production does not include creating/recording the audio narration (voiceovers), making corrections to the script post-rehearsal, resetting the stage prior to recording, or recording the lessons using Captivate (the recording time should take the exact same amount of time as the process being recorded).

What Does Production Include?

So what's left? As I mentioned on page 5, it's going to take 10 hours (on average) to produce each Captivate project. What's part of the production process?

You'll spend a lot of time working with Text Captions (you will learn about Text Captions beginning on page 48). You'll be adding interactive objects (click boxes, which you'll learn about on page 155; buttons, which you will learn about on page 99; and text entry boxes, which you will learn about on page 159) on several of your slides.

During the production process, you'll likely be adding audio clips to the project's background, individual slides and even objects on the slides.

During the production process, you'll be publishing the project into any one of several output formats and possibly uploading those files to a server (LMS) and testing for scoring or interactivity errors. After that, you'll need to fix problems you run across (don't worry, there will be plenty of problems that need to be fixed). After fixing those problems, you'll need to republish, repost and then retest.

Add it all up, and your budget looks something like this (keep in mind that the timing below does not include the time it will take to record and edit your own voice-overs or narrations):

- ❏ 40-80 hours to write a script or create the storyboard to support 12, five-minute lessons for a one-hour course.

- ❏ 120 hours to edit, produce and test 12, five-minute lessons for a one-hour eLearning course.

- ❏ 40-80 hours to write a narration script to be used by your narrator.

- ❏ Up to 100 hours to record and enhance voice narration (much less if you use Text to Speech, which you will learn about on page 137).

So there it is, a mere 400 hours (give or take) is all that stands between you and your eLearning course. Are you tired yet? No, not you... and not me. Here's the deal: while creating eLearning lessons in Captivate takes a lot of work (likely more work than you thought prior to reading the past few paragraphs), the work will actually be fun... and rewarding. I've gotten much satisfaction watching students move through my eLearning lessons and learning, and had more fun creating the lessons, than just about anything I've done in my career. I wish the same for you.

The Captivate Interface

If you use other Adobe CS5 applications, you will appreciate the familiar look and feel of Captivate's interface. When you start Captivate, you will see a menu bar at the top of the window containing just a few options (File, Edit, View, Window and Help). The Welcome Screen has an area showing recently opened projects, links for recording new projects, and Getting Started Tutorials. The interface, while remaining simple, changes as you create, open and work with projects.

Student Activity: Explore a Project

1. Read the **Note** in the margin of this page.

2. Start Adobe Captivate 5.

   The process of starting a program varies from operating system to operating system. Since Captivate is available for the Macintosh and Windows, I'll leave it to you to start Captivate using any technique you like. However, once started, Captivate is similar on all platforms. Pictured below is how Captivate appears on a computer running Windows Vista.

   As mentioned above, there are just a few menus and a Welcome Screen by default.

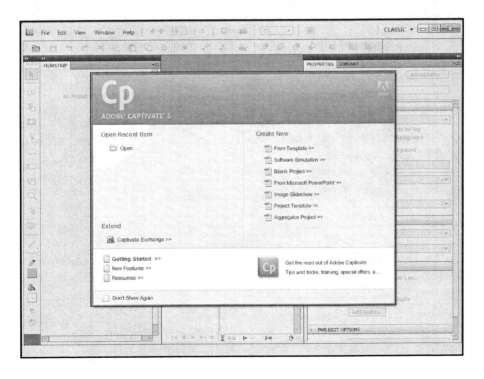

Note: You are about to open a file stored in a folder called Captivate5 EssentialsData. That folder should be located on your hard drive (C:\) if you are running Windows, or your desktop if using a Macintosh. If you have not already done so, you will need to install the data files. If necessary, complete the activity on page ix before continuing with this activity.

3. Open and preview a project.

   ❑ choose **File > Open** (or click the **Open** link from the **Open Recent Item** area on the Welcome Screen)

   The **Open** dialog box appears.

   ❑ navigate to the **Captivate5EssentialsData** folder and open **SampleProject_AceInterview.cptx**

The project opens in **Classic View**. You'll learn about Captivate's Views pretty quickly.

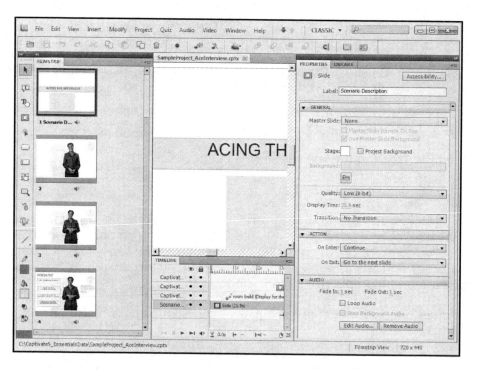

4. Close the project.

   ☐ choose **File > Close** (do not save the project if prompted)

5. Use the **Open Recent Item** area of the Welcome Screen to reopen a project.

   ☐ click **SampleProject_AceInterview** from the **Open Recent Item** area

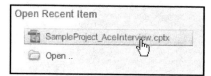

The project should once again be open and in Classic View, as shown in the picture at the top of this page.

Workspaces

As you will quickly discover, there are myriad panels and toolbars available in Captivate. Everything you see is wonderfully useful... and horribly in your way. One of the first things to learn about Captivate is that you can organize the Workspace to suit your tastes and your needs and, if you like the Workspace, you can save it for repeated use.

Student Activity: Explore the Default Workspaces

1. The SampleProject_AceInterview project should still be open.

2. Switch to the Navigation Workspace.

   ❑ click the **Workspace** menu (the menu is available where you see the word **Classic** typically found near the top right of the Captivate window)

   There are a handful of existing Workspaces including Classic, Navigation and Review.

   ❑ select **Navigation** from the Workspace drop-down menu

   The Branching window opens on your screen. Depending on how big your monitor is, the Branching window may be covering most of your Captivate project. (If the Branching window does not appear in its own window similar to what is shown below, choose **Window > Reset Navigation**.)

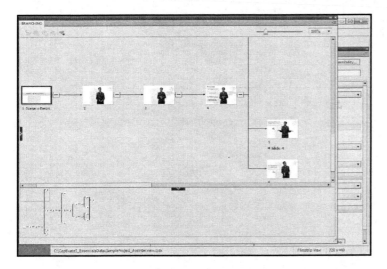

   ❑ close the Branching window (by clicking the Close button in the upper right of the window if you are using a PC or upper left if you are using a Mac)

3. Switch to the Quizzing Workspace.

   ❑ select **Quizzing** from the Workspace drop-down menu

   Switching to the Quizzing Workspace isn't nearly as dramatic as the Navigation Workspace. It appears that the only change is a Quiz Properties panel at the far left of your window.

Confidence Check

1. Still working in the SampleProject_AceInterview project, use the Workspace drop-down menu to display the **Review** Workspace.

   Notice how the Captivate window changes (there is a Comments panel in the lower right).

2. Switch to the **Applying Skin** Workspace.

   There should now be a large Skin Editor window on your screen (if not, choose **Window > Reset Applying Skin**).

3. Close the Skin Editor window.

4. Switch to the **Widget** Workspace.

   There is now a Widgets panel in the lower right.

5. Switch back to the **Classic** Workspace.

Student Activity: Modify and Reset a Workspace

1. The SampleProject_AceInterview project should still be open and you should be viewing the Classic Workspace.

   At the far right of the window there are two small icons: one is a set of two white arrows that point to the right; the other is a little menu.

2. Collapse a group to icons.

   ☐ click the white arrows (**Collapse to Icons**)

   A second ago the right side of your window contained large panels. Now, those panels have collapsed down to Icons (shown in the second picture above).

3. Expand a group to icons.

   ☐ click the arrows at the right of the Icons (**Expand Panels**)

   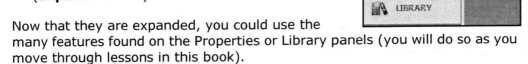

   Now that they are expanded, you could use the many features found on the Properties or Library panels (you will do so as you move through lessons in this book).

   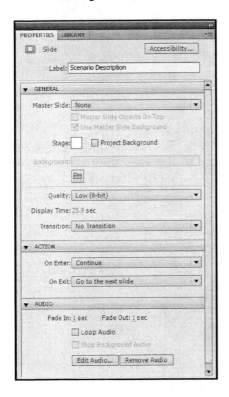

4. Close a group.

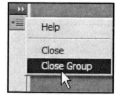

❑ at the far right of the Properties and Library panels, click the little menu (the two white arrows)

❑ choose **Close Group**

Uh oh, now you've done it. The Properties and Library panels are gone... gone! I sure hope you won't need them anytime soon, because they're not going to come back by themselves. What's that you say? I told you to close the Group? You're right, I did. Sorry about that. Ordinarily, I'd have you switch to another Workspace (like Navigation) and return to the Classic Workspace. Those pesky panels might come back. Maybe you already tried that (go ahead and try... I'll wait).

The thing about Workspaces is that they can be easily overwritten. By closing the group, you just told Captivate that this is the way you want the CLASSIC Workspace to look for you moving forward. Thankfully, you can quickly reset a Workspace back to the way it looked the first time you saw it. I'll show you how to do that next. Then I'll show you how to save any changes you make to a Workspace as your own Workspace so you can keep your custom views.

5. Reset a Workspace.

❑ with the Classic Workspace currently selected, choose **Reset 'Classic'**

Ah, that's better. The Properties and Library panels are back. Using your new "Reset" trick, you can put the panels back to the way they were should you have any regrets after changes you might make to the panels moving forward.

Student Activity: Create a Workspace

1. The SampleProject_AceInterview project should still be open and you should be viewing the reset Classic Workspace.

2. Collapse a group to icons.

   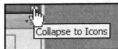

   ❑ click the **Collapse to Icons** arrows

3. Resize a panel.

   ❑ at the left side of the window, drag the right edge of the Filmstrip panel toward the left until the panel is a bit smaller

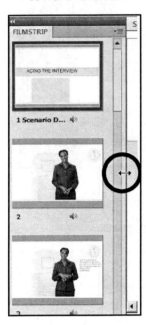

At the bottom of the window, notice that there is a panel containing several objects. This panel is known as the **Timeline**. You'll learn how to use the Timeline beginning on page 59. For now, you'll hide the Timeline so you can see more of your slides.

4. Hide the Timeline.

   ❑ choose **Window > Timeline** (to deselect the command)

Your Captivate window should look similar to the picture below.

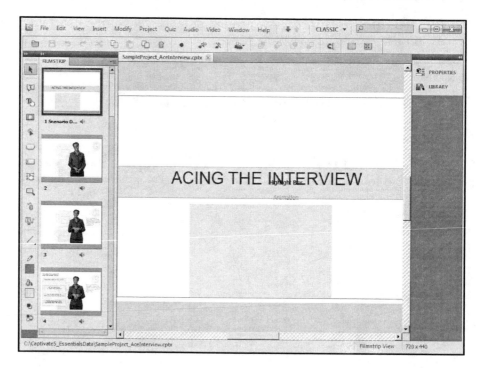

5. Create a New Workspace.

☐ from the Workspace menu, choose **New Workspace**

The New Workspace dialog box appears.

☐ type **your name Workspace** into the Name field

☐ click the **OK** button

Your new Workspace has been saved and is currently being used. The new name appears at the top of the Workspace menu.

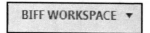

6. Switch between workspaces.

☐ from the Workspace menu, choose **Classic**

☐ from the Workspace menu, choose "your workspace"

Note: You can delete or rename a workspace by choosing Manage Workspace via the Workspace menu.

Student Activity: Navigate a Project

1. The SampleProject_AceInterview project should still be open.

2. View slides using the Filmstrip.

   ❐ scroll up or down the Filmstrip as necessary until you see **Slide 7**

   ❐ click one time on **Slide 7** to view the slide for editing

3. Jump to a slide using the Go to Slide field.

   ❐ at the top of the window, highlight the number you see in the current slide field

   ❐ type any slide number between **1** and **23**

4. Jump between slides using your keyboard.

   ❐ press either [**page up**] or [**page down**] on your keyboard

   As you press the keys, notice that you quickly move from slide to slide.

5. Jump between slides using the Next and Previous Slide arrow.

   ❐ from the top of the window, click the **Next Slide** or **Previous Slide** arrows

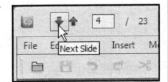

Previewing

During the lessons in this book, you will learn how to create a project from scratch, and then how to produce eLearning lessons using Captivate. At some point, you will finish the job by Publishing (you will learn how to Publish beginning on page 187). Prior to Publishing, it's a great idea to Preview the lesson so you can see how it will look once published. There are five Preview options: Play Slide, Project, From this Slide, Next 5 Slides and In Web Browser. Among them, I've found Project and Next 5 Slides to be the two Preview modes I rely on the most.

Student Activity: Preview a Project

1. The SampleProject_AceInterview project should still be open.

2. Preview the project.

    ☐ click the **Preview** tool 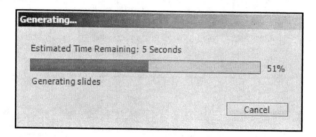 and choose **Project** (or choose **File > Preview > Project**)

The project is generated and the lesson begins to play.

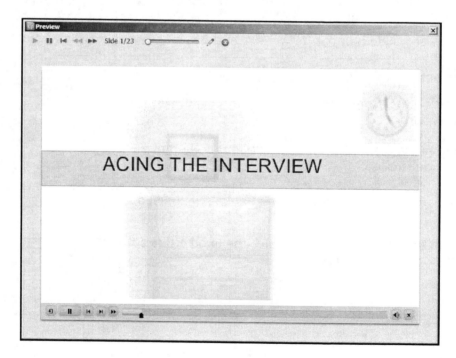

3. Spend a moment watching the lesson and interacting with the screens when prompted. As you move through the activities in this book, you will learn how to create lessons with features similar to those in this project.

   There are two playbars you can use to skip ahead through the lesson. One is located at the top of the window; a second is located at the bottom of the window. The top playbar will not appear when you Publish the project—it's there for you as the developer. The bottom playbar is what your learners will see (and use) when the project is published.

4. When you are finished interacting with the lesson (you do not need to watch the entire thing), click the **End** button located at the top of the window.

Student Activity: Zoom Closer to a Slide

1. The SampleProject_AceInterview project should still be open.

2. Go to any slide in the project.

3. Zoom away from the slide.

   ❑ find the **Zoom** drop-down menu at the top of the window

   ❑ select **50** from the Zoom drop-down menu (or choose **View > Magnification > 50%**)

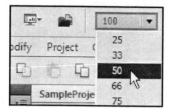

   You can zoom as far away as 25%, and as up close and personal as 400%.

4. Change the slide zoom to Best Fit.

   ❑ select **Best Fit** from the Zoom drop-down menu

   Depending on the size of the Captivate window, Best Fit is typically the best view for working on a slide.

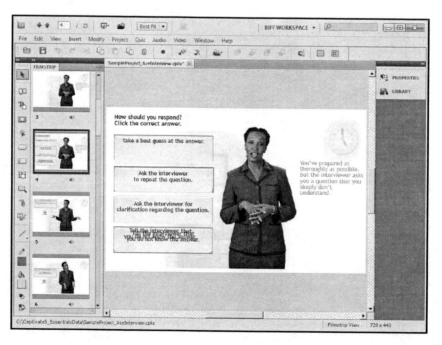

5. Close the project (there is no need to save if prompted).

iCONLOGiC

"Skills and Drills" Learning

Module 2: Recording Demos and Sims

In This Module You Will Learn About:

- Resolution and Recording Size, page 20
- The Development Process, page 21
- Preparing to Record, page 23
- Demonstrations, page 29
- Assessment Simulations, page 34
- Training Simulations, page 37
- Custom Recordings, page 40

And You Will Learn To:

- Rehearse a Script, page 24
- Edit Recording Settings, page 25
- Set Recording Keys, page 27
- Record a Demonstration, page 29
- Record an Assessment, page 34
- Record a Training Simulation, page 37
- Record a Custom Simulation, page 41

Resolution and Recording Size

During this module you will learn how to use Adobe Captivate to record a software demonstration and then a software simulation (you will learn the difference between a demonstration and simulation as you move through the lessons that follow).

During the recording process, you will perform a few commands on your computer and, provided Captivate is running and recording, every click you make with your mouse will result in one screen capture (also known as a screen shot).

Prior to recording, you should be aware of two things that control how sharp and how large your Captivate screen captures will be: Display Resolution and Recording Area.

Display Resolution

A computer monitor is measured in pixels (a pixel is a little square that is the basic component of any computer graphic). If a monitor is set to show more pixels, it is known as increasing the resolution. At a higher resolution, graphics and text will look sharper, but smaller. The fewer pixels you request, the lower the resolution, and the larger the screen elements appear.

Consider the following Web browser statistics (compiled by **www.w3schools.com/browsers/browsers_stats.asp**): First, Firefox is currently the most popular Web browser (with just under 47% of the market; Internet Explorer is second at 31%; and the newest entry, Google Chrome, is up and coming with just under 16%). Second, the trend in monitor display resolution is 1024x768 pixels (48% of computer users use this setting while 30% use a higher setting).

If your computer is set to a high resolution (such as 1280x1024) when you record screen captures using Adobe Captivate, a customer viewing your published project at a lower display resolution (such as 800x600) will have to scroll significantly to see the action you recorded.

In contrast, if your computer is set to a lower display resolution (such as 1024x768) when you record your project, a customer with a higher screen resolution will have no trouble viewing your project. However, if you record your projects at the lower screen resolution, you may not be happy with the appearance of the screen icons and fonts (they may be too big and not as sharp as they would appear at the higher screen resolution). I know what you're thinking, "So many display resolution concerns, so little time!" I'd like to say that display resolution is your only worry. Sorry, there's more. How big of a Recording Area are you going to use?

Recording Area

The Recording Area is not the same thing as Display Resolution (although the two settings are constantly confused). The Display Resolution is controlled via your computer's Display settings.

In contrast, the physical Recording Area is set from within Captivate and is the physical amount of the screen that you will be capturing during the recording process. There are several preset sizes available within Captivate from 208x176 up to 1024x768, and you can specify your own.

With so many choices, what should you do? I recommend that you set your computer's Display Resolution to 1024x768. In addition, I recommend a Captivate Recording Area of no larger than 800x600 if possible.

The Development Process

I agree with people who say that Captivate is a very easy program to learn and use. Compared with programs like Adobe Photoshop, learning Captivate is easy. In fact, you'll have the Captivate basics pretty much figured out in two days or less (that's the time it should take you to finish this book). However, there's a whole development process you need to go through if you intend to produce effective eLearning (also known as Computer Based Training or CBTs), and Captivate mastery is only a small part of that process. Getting a handle on the eLearning development process isn't easy. It takes a lot of practice, experience and, above all, patience.

I've listed the typical eLearning development process below. This list includes a skill level number indicating the level of difficulty for each task. The numbers go from 1 to 10, with 10 indicating the most difficult task.

- ❐ **Write It:** If you're not a writer, you'll need someone to write the step-by-step instructions (also known as a script or storyboard) necessary to record the project in Captivate. You'll typically find technical writers doing this kind of work, and I consider this the most important process. Without a good script, you don't have a movie. Think I'm kidding? What do *Battlefield Earth*, *Barb Wire*, *Godzilla*, *Heaven's Gate*, *Popeye* and *Ishtar* have in common? *(Skill Level: 10)*

- ❐ **Rehearse It:** Take the completed script and go through it with the software you'll be recording in front of you. Don't skip any steps. You'll be able to see if the steps you wrote are incomplete or inaccurate before you attempt to record the movie in Captivate. *(Skill Level: 2)*

- ❐ **Reset It:** After rehearsing the steps, be sure to "undo" everything you did. Few things are more frustrating than recording your movie only to find a step you intend to demonstrate has already been performed.
(Skill Level: 1)

- ❐ **Record It:** If rehearsals went well, the recording process should as well. *(Skill Level: 1)*

- ❐ **Clean It:** This is where you use Captivate to add highlight boxes, captions, text entry fields, buttons, click boxes, animation, question slides, audio, etc. If the project is large and each slide needs your attention, you should budget 7-10 hours to get the project "cleaned." *(Skill Level: 8)*

- ❐ **Publish It:** While not a difficult task, if your project is large this could take a great deal of time. You cannot do any work in Captivate while your project is publishing.
(Skill Level: 1)

- ❐ **Post It:** This is a broad category. Posting your project will mean different things depending on where your finished lessons are supposed to go. For instance, if your lessons are supposed to end up inside a Learning Management System (LMS), you will have to set up the reporting features for your project, Publish the project and then upload or install it into the LMS. After the lesson has been uploaded, you will need to test the lesson to ensure that it scores as expected. If you plan to simply add the lessons to your Web site, Posting may be as simple as using Captivate's FTP feature to upload the lesson files to your Web server. *(Skill Level: 2 or 3... or higher if your LMS is difficult to use)*

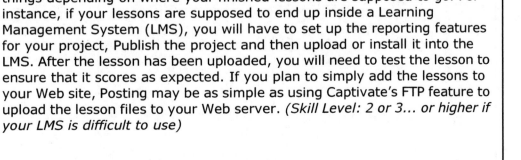

❐ **Test It:** This task isn't difficult, but it could take time. If you find a problem, you've got to go back and clean it, publish it and retest it. Some people argue that this step belongs above the Publish It process. I cannot argue with that logic. However, after testing the project, you'll still need to Publish it and, as I mentioned above, if you're working with an LMS, upload it and test again. Maybe it should be Test It, Publish It, Test It. See how easy I am? *(Skill Level: 2)*

❐ **Republish, Repost, Retest:** If something didn't work when you tested the posted version of your lesson, you'll have to return to Captivate and fix the problem. After that, you'll Publish, Post and Test again. While this may not be a difficult process, it could take time. *(Skill Level: 2 or 3... or higher if you can't resolve the problem)*

Preparing to Record

Captivate projects consist of slides, similar to Microsoft PowerPoint. You can create a blank Captivate project and insert slides, just like PowerPoint. If you need pictures of a software application, you can use any one of several programs to create screen captures. For instance, I use SnagIt (**www.snagit.com**) and FullShot (**www.fullshot.com**) all the time. In fact, FullShot was used to create most of the screen captures shown throughout this book. Any screen captures you create using a screen capture application can easily be inserted onto a slide as a background image.

However, most people who create Captivate projects elect to use Captivate to create the screen captures. When using Captivate to create the screen captures, there are two recording types: Auto Recording and Manual Recording.

If you create projects using the Manual Recording type, you are responsible for pressing a specific key on your keyboard each time you want Captivate to create a screen capture (the default key is the Print Screen key). The problem with recording projects using the Manual Recording method is that you'll have to be diligent about pressing a key (or combination of keys) on your keyboard. You could easily get distracted and forget to capture important screens.

If you use Captivate's Auto Recording mode, Captivate automatically captures the steps you take on your computer by creating a screen capture every time you click your mouse (you can left click or right click to get a screen capture). There are four capture modes: Demonstration, Assessment Simulation, Training Simulation and Custom. Each of the modes will be covered during this module.

Rehearsals

As mentioned on page 21, the Write It phase, or script development phase, is the most important and difficult part of the eLearning development process. After the Write It phase, you should rehearse the script to ensure that the script is accurate.

Here's the scenario: you have been hired to create an eLearning course that will teach new employees how to use the corporate Help System. One of the lessons will include navigating the Help System.

The following example shows the kind of step-by-step script you might create or receive from a Subject Matter Expert (SME). The steps detail how to move through a process (in this case, the process entails clicking some simple navigation buttons in a Help System):

```
Steps to record in Captivate:

    1. Click the Index button.

    2. Click the Search button.

    3. Click the Glossary button.

    4. Click the Contents button.

    5. Stop recording.
```

The script above sounds simple. However, you will not know what kind of trouble you are going to get into unless you step through the script prior to recording in Captivate. Let's go ahead and run a rehearsal.

Student Activity: Rehearse a Script

1. Minimize (hide) Captivate.

2. Open the **Captivate5EssentialsData** folder and then open the **PoliciesProcedures** folder.

   The **PoliciesProcedures** folder contains a Help System created with Adobe RoboHelp. This Help System is actually a Policies and Procedures manual for a company called South River Technologies. You will be using this Help System to practice, and then record, the process of using the navigation buttons (Content, Index, Search and Glossary).

3. Open the Help System's Start Page

   ❏ from within the PoliciesProcedures folder, open **index.htm**

   The index.htm file is the start page for the entire Help System (which opens in your default Web browser).

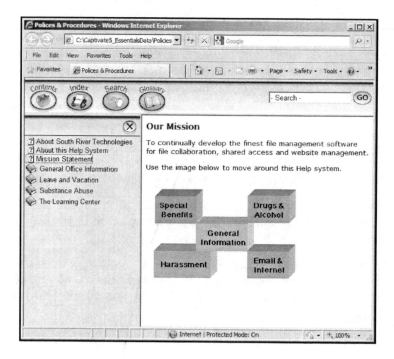

4. Rehearse the script.

   ❏ click the **Index** button near the top of the browser window

   ❏ click the **Search** button near the top of the browser window

   ❏ click the **Glossary** button near the top of the browser window

   ❏ click the **Contents** button near the top of the browser window

   Hey, look at that! The script worked perfectly... no surprises. You are now ready to record these exact steps. Only this time, it's for real. Captivate will create a screen capture for you each time you click your mouse.

Student Activity: Edit Recording Settings

1. Set Audio Options.

    ❏ leave the index file open in your Web browser and return to Captivate

    ❏ if you are using a PC, choose **Edit > Preferences**; if you are using a Mac, choose **Adobe Captivate > Preferences**

    The Preferences dialog box opens. There are two main categories at the left: Global and Recording.

    ❏ from the **Recording** category, select **Settings**

    There are several options available in the Recording area.

    ❏ from the Generate Captions In area, ensure that **English** is selected from the drop-down menu

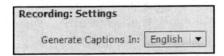

    ❏ from the Audio Options area, deselect **Narration** and **Actions in Real Time** if necessary; leave **Camera Sounds** selected

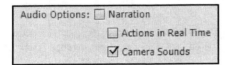

    The **Narration** option allows you to record a narrator at the same time that you record the lesson. Because you will not be using audio for the lesson you just rehearsed, you won't need this option. However, this feature could prove useful if you are relying on a subject matter expert to both record the lesson and provide the narration. Instead of creating the lesson and the narration on different days, both can be created at the same time. Nevertheless, I typically work with professional audio talent and import audio files into my Captivate projects later during production (you will work with audio on page 124).

    If you select **Actions in Real Time**, Captivate will set the slide timing for your project slides to match the time it took you to complete a process.
    For instance, if you waited 10 seconds from one click to the next, Captivate would set your slide timing to match. I typically do not use this feature.

    With **Camera Sounds** selected, you will hear a sound much like a camera shutter every time Captivate creates a screen capture.

2. Disable keystroke sounds.

    ❏ from the Audio Options area, deselect **Keystrokes** and **Hear Keyboard Tap Sounds**

    If you leave **Keystrokes** selected, Captivate will create a mini movie within your project that literally shows what you type, as you're typing—typos and all. I typically do not use this feature. Instead, I allow users to type text

directly into my Captivate simulations using Text Entry Boxes. You will learn about Text Entry Boxes on page 159.

3. Set the Hide options.

❐ from the Hide area, deselect **Recording Window**, **Task Icon** and **System Tray Icon** (Mac users, deselect **Recording Window** and **Dock Icon**)

Hide: ☐ Recording Window	PC at the left, Mac at the	Hide: ☐ Recording Window
☐ Task Icon	right.	
☐ System Tray Icon		☐ Dock Icon

If you had selected Recording Window, Task Icon (Dock Icon) and System Tray Icon, you would hide all evidence of Captivate during the capture process. These items would only get in the way if you were capturing your desktop and the Captivate application icon was on the screen. Since I tend to create software simulations within specific application windows, I typically leave these three options deselected.

4. Ensure that new windows always appear in the Recording Area.

❐ from the Others area, ensure **Move New Windows Inside Recording Area** is selected

The **Move New Windows Inside Recording Area** option could prove useful if a pesky window tried to appear outside of your recording area. In that case, Captivate would automatically move the window into your Recording Area. Without this feature, you would have to pause the movie, drag the window into the Recording Area and continue. I typically enable this feature.

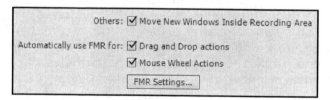

5. Enable FMR.

❐ from the Automatically use FMR for area, ensure both **Drag and Drop actions** and **Mouse Wheel Actions** are selected

These final two options deal with Full Motion Recordings (FMR), which you will learn more about on page 198. Generally speaking, FMRs are useful when you want to demonstrate a complex mouse motion. During the recording process, clicking your mouse will create a single screen shot. However, if you drag your mouse instead of simply clicking, Captivate will create a full motion clip (an animation within a slide).

❐ click the **OK** button

Student Activity: Set Recording Keys

1. Customize a recording key.

   ☐ if you are using a PC, choose **Edit > Preferences**; if you are using a Mac, choose **Adobe Captivate > Preferences**

   The Preferences dialog box reopens.

   ☐ from the **Recording** category, select **Keys**

   ☐ click in the **To Stop Recording** field and press the "**y**" key on your keyboard

   The letter "y" replaces the key that was in the field by default.

Recording: Keys
General:
To Stop Recording: Y
To Pause/Resume Recording: Pause

   If you were to move forward and record a lesson using Captivate, you would press "y' on your keyboard to end the recording process. You could customize the fields in this dialog box to suit your needs (a useful option, especially if there is a program on your keyboard that is running and conflicts with the keys listed here). However, for most people, the default keys work wonderfully.

2. Reset the default Recording Keys.

   ☐ with the Preferences dialog box still showing (Edit or Adobe Captivate menu), and **Keys** selected from the Recording Category, click the **Restore Defaults** button

   Restore Defaults

   Mac users: Consider changing the "To Stop Recording" key to [**End**] so that the instructions used in this book match your system. If you cannot find the [**End**] key on your keyboard (some Mac keyboards simply do not have an [**End**] key), leave the defaults as is. However, make a note of the keys you will need to press and keep in mind that instructions to stop the recording process will be referenced as the [**End**] key in this book.

General:
To Stop Recording: End

   ☐ click the **OK** button

   PC users, Hold on tight, you are now ready to record your first video.
   (Mac users, you'll need to complete one more chore on the next page.)

Access for Assistive Devices

If you are using a Macintosh and attempt to record a video you'll likely run face-first into a dialog box instructing you to Enable Access for Assistive Devices. To avoid the stress of seeing that dialog box just as you're ready to record your first lesson, let's go ahead and enable the feature.

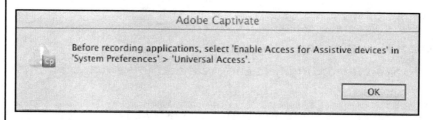

Note: The following activity is for Mac users only (PC users can move to the "Record a Demonstration" activity that begins on page 29).

Student Activity: Enable Access for Assistive Devices

1. Enable access for assistive devices.

    ❏ from the Apple menu, choose **System Preferences**

    The System Preferences window opens.

    ❏ from the **System** group, double-click the **Universal Access** button

    The Universal Access window opens.

    ❏ select **Enable access for assistive devices**

    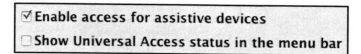

    ❏ close the Universal Access window

    And now you can hold on tight too... you are now ready to record your first video.

2. Return to Adobe Captivate (if necessary).

Demonstrations

There are generally two types of lessons you can record using Adobe Captivate: demonstrations and simulations. A demonstration is ideal if you want to show a quick software concept to a customer, but you don't expect the customer to follow along and actually perform the steps being demonstrated. Demonstration mode automatically includes captions, Highlight Boxes and mouse movements.

Student Activity: Record a Demonstration

1. Captivate should be running (no projects should be open). In addition, the index.htm file should still be open in your Web browser.

   Note: If you have forgotten about the **index.htm** file or you closed it, you should reopen it now (the file is located in the PoliciesProcedures folder).

2. Display the Recording Area and control panel.

   ☐ select **Software Simulation** from the Create New area of the Welcome Screen (or choose **File > Record new project**)

   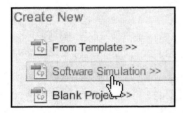

   On your computer display, notice two things besides the browser window. First, there is a large red box known as the **Recording Area**. Second, there is a control panel containing Size and Recording Type areas.

   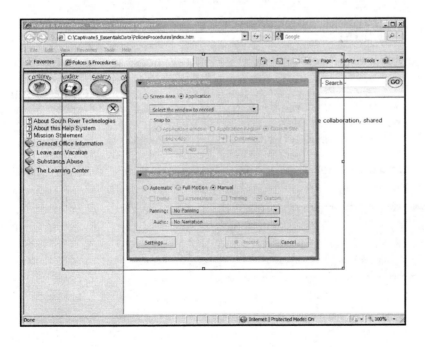

3. Select the Policies & Procedures window as the Application.

❑ from the top of the control panel, select **Application**

❑ from the drop-down menu that appears beneath Application, select **Policies & Procedures** that is open in the browser

4. Specify a recording size.

❑ from the Snap to area, select **Custom Size**

❑ from the next drop-down menu, select **640 x 480**

I discussed the best size for your Recording Area back on page 20. In reality, you should use the smallest Recording Size that works for you and the program you are recording (keeping in mind that the smaller your recording area, the smaller your finished video will be). In this instance, 640 x 480 will work just fine.

Notice that the Policies & Procedures window has been resized to 640 x 480 and is fitting perfectly within the red Recording Area.

5. Select a Recording Mode.

❑ from the Recording Type area of the Control panel, select **Automatic**

With this option selected, every click of your mouse during the recording process will create a screen capture. In contrast, had you selected Manual mode, you would need to press a key on your keyboard (typically the [print screen] key) to capture the screen.

❑ select **Demo** from the list of modes and ensure that the remaining three options are **deselected**

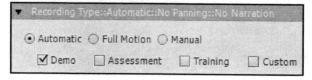

6. Disable Panning and Audio Narration.

   ❏ ensure that Panning is set to **No Panning** and that Audio is set to **No Narration**

   You'll learn about Panning later (page 202).

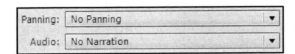

7. Check the Demo settings.

   ❏ click the **Settings** button

   The Preferences dialog box appears again. The **Modes** category is already selected.

   ❏ ensure that Demonstration is selected in the Mode drop-down menu

   ❏ from the bottom of the dialog box, click the **Restore Defaults** button

   The Demonstration that you are about to record will automatically **Add Text Captions**, **Show Mouse Location and Movement** and add a **Highlight Boxes on Click**.

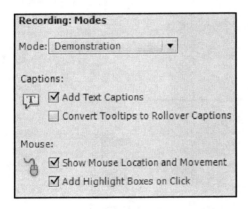

   ❏ click the **OK** button

8. Record a Demonstration.

   ❏ click the **Record** button

   You will see a three-second countdown and then nothing.

   While nothing seems to have happened, Captivate is now *watching* you and waiting to take screen captures. All that's required now is for you to click as appropriate.

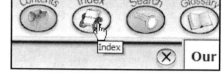

❑ using your mouse, click the **Index** button in the Help window

And just like that, one simple little click by you, and Captivate has created a screen capture. Easy huh? Let's do some more!

❑ click the **Search** button

Another screen capture is taken.

❑ click the **Glossary** button

Another screen capture is taken.

❑ click the **Contents** button to capture a final screen

9. Stop the recording.

❑ press [**end**] on your keyboard (or the key you specified on page 27 as your keyboard shortcut to stop the recording process—the default for the Mac is [**Command**] [**Enter**]... not [Command] [Return])

Once you stop the recording process, slides are created and an unsaved project opens in Captivate.

10. Load the Workspace you created back on page 13.

Your window should look similar to this (Mac users, review the note on the next page):

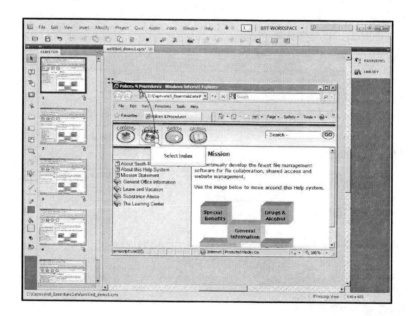

11. Save the project.

❑ choose **File > Save**

❑ name the project **UseNavBar1** (save the project to the **Captivate5EssentialsData** folder)

Note: If you can't get Captivate to stop recording via your keyboard shortcut, you can always manually stop the recording process by clicking the Captivate icon in the System Tray (PC users) or the Dock (Mac users).

12. Preview the project.

   ☐ choose **File > Preview > Project**

   As the preview plays, notice that the project contains text captions and Highlight Boxes. You will learn how to create captions from scratch as you move through the lessons in this book. If this is your first time automatically recording an eLearning project, there is a good chance you have just been blown away with the fact that Captivate added reasonable, usable text to your new lesson out of the box. *Very cool!*

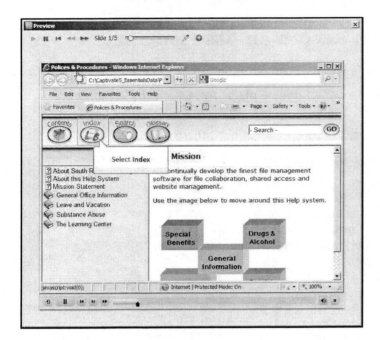

Mac users: The captions that are automatically created are probably not as helpful as the one shown in the picture above. In the image at the right, the caption, which was created using the Mac version of Captivate, says "Click the Toolbar scroller area," which isn't as nice as the caption created on the PC side. For whatever reason, the Mac browsers don't appreciate the Policies Help System as much as PC browsers do. No worries. The captions that are created are 100% editable. You will learn about inserting and editing captions beginning on page 48.

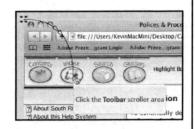

Moving forward, consider recording something a little different than what you are asked to record during the remaining activities in this module. For instance, record the process of going to Google and changing the Language settings (click **Language Tools**, under **My Language**, click where it says **English** and select a different language from the list). In this instance, the captions created by Captivate for the Macintosh were much more helpful.

13. When the preview is finished, close the preview by pressing the [**Esc**] key on your keyboard.

14. Save and then close the project.

Assessment Simulations

Assessment Simulations are used to create interactive eLearning lessons. Using this mode, you'll end up with a lesson that includes Click Boxes (to make the lesson interactive) and Failure Captions (that will help the user who clicks in the wrong place or performs the wrong step). However, an Assessment Simulation won't include Text Captions (the elements that tell users what to do or explain a concept). As a result, an Assessment Simulation works best when teamed with a Demonstration lesson. In short, you would need two Captivate projects for every lesson: one to explain and demonstrate the key concepts; another to assess the learner.

Student Activity: Record an Assessment

1. Set the Preferences for the Assessment Simulations you are about to record.

   ❏ if you are using a PC, choose **Edit > Preferences**; Mac users, choose **Adobe Captivate > Preferences**

   ❏ from the **Recording** category, select **Modes**

   ❏ from the Mode drop-down menu, select **Assessment Simulation**

   ❏ click the **Restore Defaults** button at the bottom of the dialog box

Since this type of lesson is supposed to assess a learner's comprehension of a Demonstration they have theoretically just watched, you would not need text captions to explain what the learner is supposed to do. By default, an Assessment Simulation will include Click Boxes (hot spots) that the learner will need to click to move to the next slide in the assessment. The Click Boxes will include Failure Captions (captions that will appear should the learner click in the wrong place). Text Entry Boxes, also selected by default, are a very nice feature which you will learn about on page 159.

   ❏ click the **OK** button

2. Record an Assessment Simulation.

   ❏ from the Create New area of the Welcome Screen, click **Software Simulation** (or choose **File > Record new project**)

The Recording Area and control panel appear again.

Recording: Modes

Mode: | Assessment Simulation ▼ |

Captions:
[T] ☐ Add Text Captions
☐ Convert Tooltips to Rollover Captions

Mouse:
🖱 ☐ Show Mouse Location and Movement
☐ Add Highlight Boxes on Click

Click Boxes:
☀ ☑ Add Click Boxes on Mouse Click
☐ Success Caption ☑ Failure Caption
☐ Hint Caption ☐ Limit Attempts to 2
☐ Show Hand Cursor on the Click Box

Text Entry Boxes:
[I] ☑ Automatically Add Text Entry Boxes for Text Fields
☐ Success Caption ☑ Failure Caption
☐ Hint Caption ☐ Limit Attempts to 2

Restore Defaults

---

3. Select the Policies & Procedures browser window as the Application.

❏ from the top of the control panel, select **Application** (if necessary)

❏ from the drop-down menu that appears beneath Application, select **Policies & Procedures** (if necessary)

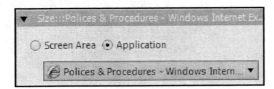

4. Specify a recording size.

❏ from the Snap to area, select **Custom Size** (if necessary)

❏ from the next drop-down menu, ensure that **640 x 480** is selected

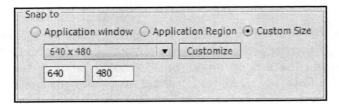

5. Select a Recording Mode.

❏ from the Recording Type area of the Control panel, select **Automatic**

❏ select **Assessment** from the list of modes and ensure that the remaining three options are **deselected**

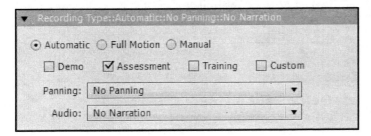

6. Disable Panning and Audio Narration.

❏ ensure Panning is set to **No Panning** and that Audio is set to **No Narration**

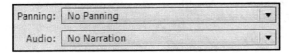

7. Record the Assessment Simulation.

   ❏ click the **Record** button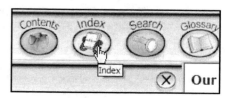

   ❏ once the Countdown goes away, use your mouse to click the **Index** button in the Help window

   ❏ click the **Search** button

   ❏ click the **Glossary** button

   ❏ click the **Contents** button

8. Stop the recording.

   ❏ press [**end**] on your keyboard press [**end**] on your keyboard (or the key you specified on page 27 as your keyboard shortcut to stop the recording process—the default for the Mac is [**Command**] [**Enter**]... not [Command] [Return])

Note: If you can't get Captivate to stop recording via your keyboard shortcut, you can always manually stop the recording process by clicking the Captivate icon in the System Tray (PC users) or the Dock (Mac users).

Once you press [**end**] on your keyboard, the recording process is terminated, slides are created and the unsaved video opens in Captivate. On the first slide of the project, notice that there is an object positioned over the Index button on the slide—this is the Click Box that was created automatically during the recording process. There is also a Failure Caption (the exact appearance of the text and the text caption is not important at this time).

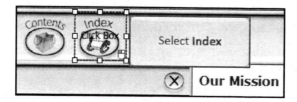

9. Save the project.

   ❏ choose **File > Save**

   ❏ name the project **UseNavBar2** and save it to the **Captivate5EssentialsData** folder

10. Preview the project.

    ❏ choose **File > Preview > Project**

    As the preview begins, the lesson appears to freeze. Because you recorded an Assessment Simulation, the lesson is actually waiting for interaction from you.

    ❏ click in the middle of the window

    Because you were actually supposed to click on the Index button on the Navigation bar, a Failure Caption appears urging you to select Index. Your learners will see Failure Captions whenever they click someplace they aren't supposed to in error.

11. Continue to interact with the simulation. When finished, close the Preview.

12. Save and then close the project.

Training Simulations

Training Simulations are very similar to Assessment Simulations. However, in addition to Click Boxes and Failure Captions being automatically added, you will also gain **Hint Captions**—captions that appear if the learner gets close to the Click Box (hot spot) but does not actually click on the Click Box.

Student Activity: Record a Training Simulation

1. Set the Preferences for the Training Assessment you are about to record.

   ❒ if you are using a PC, choose **Edit > Preferences**; Mac users, choose **Adobe Captivate > Preferences**

   ❒ from the **Recording** category, select **Modes**

   ❒ from the Mode drop-down menu, select **Training Simulation**

   ❒ click the **Restore Defaults** button at the bottom of the dialog box

As mentioned above, a Training Simulation is identical to an Assessment Simulation with one difference—Hint Captions will be added to the recording. If your learners get close to the hot spot but neglect to click, the Hint Captions will guide them.

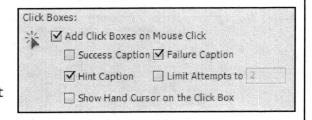

   ❒ click the **OK** button

2. Record a Training Simulation.

   ❒ from the Create New area of the Welcome Screen, click **Software Simulation**

The Recording Area and control panel appear again.

3. Select the Policies & Procedures window as the Application.

   ❒ from the top of the control panel, select **Application** (if necessary)

   ❒ from the drop-down menu that appears beneath Application, choose **Policies & Procedures** (if necessary)

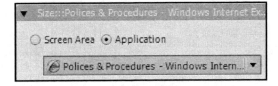

4. Specify a recording size.

❏ from the Snap to area, select **Custom Size** (if necessary)

❏ from the next drop-down menu, ensure that **640 x 480** is selected

5. Select a Recording Mode.

❏ from the Recording Type area of the Control panel, select **Automatic** (if necessary)

❏ select **Training** from the list of modes and ensure that the remaining three modes are **deselected**

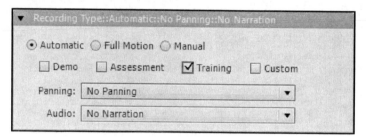

6. Disable Panning and Audio Narration.

❏ ensure that Panning is set to **No Panning** and that Audio is set to **No Narration**

7. Record the Assessment Simulation.

❏ click the **Record** button

❏ once the Countdown goes away, use your mouse to click the **Index** button in the Help window

❏ click the **Search** button

❏ click the **Glossary** button

❏ click the **Contents** button

8. Stop the recording.

❏ press [**end**] on your keyboard

As with an Assessment Simulation, you'll notice on the first slide of the project that there is a Click Box positioned over the Index button on the slide. As before, there is also a Failure Caption. But you will also notice that there is a Hint Caption.

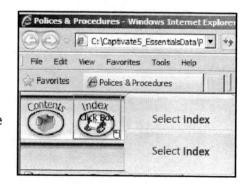

9. Save the project.

  ❏ choose **File > Save**

  ❏ name the project **UseNavBar3** and save it to the **Captivate5EssentialsData** folder

10. Interact with the training lesson.

  ❏ choose **File > Preview > Project**

As with the Assessment Simulation you created during the last activity, the lesson appears to be frozen. This lesson is waiting for you to interact with it.

  ❏ click in the middle of the window

A Failure Caption appears urging you to click the Index button.

  ❏ move your mouse close to the Index button (but don't click)

You should see a "hint" caption. As a reminder, both the Hint Captions and Failure Captions were automatically created for you because of the default settings for a Training Assessment recording mode.

11. Spend a moment interacting with the lesson.

12. When finished, close the preview.

13. Save and close the project.

Custom Recordings

You have now learned how to record three kinds of eLearning lessons with Captivate: Demonstrations (page 29), Assessment Simulations (page 34) and Training Simulations (page 37). Between demonstrations and simulations, which type of lesson will result in the most effective learning experience for your users? Good question—and there is no clear-cut answer. Demonstrations are relatively quick and easy to create. However, demonstrations do not allow for learner interaction. By watching a demonstration, without the ability to interact with it, the potential for learning is reduced.

The Text Captions that are automatically created by Captivate are great, but they are written in the active voice. For instance, a typical Text Caption is likely to contain the words "Select the File Menu." Upon reading that text, a learner is likely to take the caption's instructions literally and attempt to select the File menu. Unfortunately, at the same time that the learner is trying to interact with the simulation, the cursor that Captivate created when the lesson was recorded is also moving across the screen. The result could be confusion for the learner.

Simulations are perfect for assessing what a learner has absorbed during a demonstration. Since Simulations do not add any Text Captions by default, there are no instructions telling the learner what to do. The learner will either perform the required steps or click somewhere on the screen and see a Failure Caption when they perform the process incorrectly.

Many Captivate developers create both a Demonstration and a Simulation. That's all well and good until you remember that it could take several hours to produce the lessons. If you elect to produce both a Demonstration and an Assessment, you could make twice the work for yourself.

Demonstration or Simulation: Which Mode is Best?

Instead of creating a Demonstration and a Simulation, I recommend you record a custom, or hybrid, lesson that incorporates the best of the Demonstration, Assessment and Training modes.

When you are finished recording the hybrid movie, you will end up with a lesson that bridges the gap between a Demonstration and Assessment/Simulation lesson. You will also discover that the captions created by Captivate are written in the active voice and encourage learner participation.

Student Activity: Record a Custom Simulation

1. Set the Preferences for the simulation you are about to record.

    ☐ if you are using a PC, choose **Edit > Preferences**; Mac users, choose **Adobe Captivate > Preferences**

    ☐ from the **Recording** category, select **Modes**

    ☐ from the Mode drop-down menu, select **Custom**

    ☐ click the **Restore Defaults** button at the bottom of the dialog box

    ☐ from the Captions area, select **Add Text Captions**

    ☐ from the Click Boxes area, select **Add Click Boxes on Mouse Click**

    ☐ select **Failure Captions**

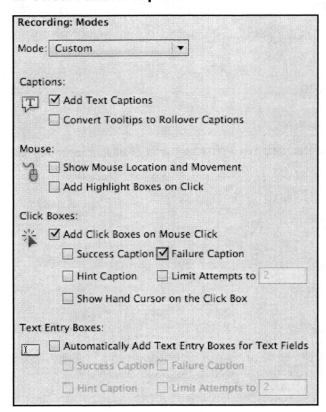

By now you should be somewhat comfortable with the available options in this dialog box. You have selected **Add Text Captions** so that the captions will be created for you. *Nice.* And, since the captions are written in the active voice, you may be able to use them in the new lesson with little editing. *Nicer.* Everything else has been left deselected except for **Click Boxes** and **Failure Captions**. As a result, this will be a highly interactive simulation. *Nicest!*

☐ click the **OK** button

2. Record the custom simulation.

❏ from the Create New area of the Welcome Screen, click **Software Simulation**

❏ from the top of the control panel, select **Application** (if necessary)

❏ from the drop-down menu that appears beneath Application, select **Policies & Procedures** (if necessary)

3. Specify a recording size.

❏ from the Snap to area, select **Custom Size** (if necessary)

❏ from the next drop-down menu, select **640 x 480** (if necessary)

4. Select a Recording Mode.

❏ from the Recording Type area of the Control panel, select **Automatic** (if necessary)

❏ select **Custom** from the list of modes and ensure that the remaining three modes are **deselected**

5. Disable Panning and Audio Narration.

❏ ensure that Panning is set to **No Panning** and that Audio is set to **No Narration**

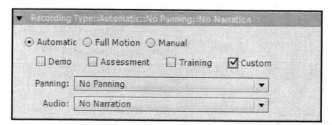

6. Record the Custom simulation.

❏ click the **Record** button and, once the Countdown goes away, use your mouse to click the **Index** button in the Help window

❏ click the **Search** button, click the **Glossary** button and then click the **Contents** button

7. Stop the recording by pressing [**End**] on your keyboard.

8. Save the project to the **Captivate5EssentialsData** folder as **UseNavBar4**.

9. Preview the project. (**File > Preview**)

As you move through the lesson, notice that the Text Captions are written in the active voice. Also notice that there are Click Boxes (hot spots) in the correct place that make this lesson 100 percent interactive.

10. When finished previewing the lesson, close the preview and then save and close the project.

Confidence Check

During the steps that follow you will first get a chance to record a Demonstration project that creates captions in languages other than English. Then you will record projects in multiple modes, at one time.

Record a lesson using a different language other than English:

1. Display the Preferences dialog box.

2. Select **Settings** from the Recording Category.

3. Select any language you'd like from the **Generate Captions In** drop-down menu.

Note: If you do not have the Asian fonts installed on your computer, you might want to select a language other than the Asian languages. Without the Asian fonts, you'll see white boxes instead of letters in the resulting Text Captions.

4. Click the **OK** button.

5. Create a new Software Simulation.

6. Select the Policies & Procedures window as the Application and the **640x480** size.

7. Select **Demo** as the mode and ensure that all of the other modes are deselected.

8. Click **Record** and then run through the same script you have used throughout this module (click each of the navigation buttons near the top of the Help window).

9. End the recording process.

10. Save the project as **UseNavBar_Language** (save the project to the Captivate5EssentialsData folder).

11. Preview the project.

    Notice that the Text Captions are using the language you specified in the **Generate Captions In** drop-down menu. *How cool is that?*

    Hold on to your hat, things are about to get even cooler!

12. When finished with the preview, save and then close the project.

13. Display the **Captivate Preferences** dialog box again and set the **Generate Captions In** language back to **English**.

14. Create a new Software Simulation. However, just prior to recording the new lesson, select **all 4 modes** (Demonstration, Assessment, Training and Custom) from the Recording Type area.

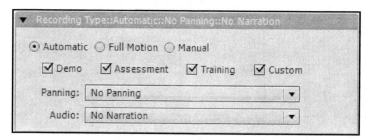

15. Record the process of clicking on the Help System's navigation buttons one final time and then End the recording process.

    Notice that four projects are created and opened at one time (you can see the four unsaved projects are open via their tabs at the top of the window):

    You can switch between open projects by clicking the project's tab.

16. Close each of the projects (there is no need to save any of them).

17. Close the Web browser and return to Captivate.

iCONLOGiC

"Skills and Drills" Learning

Module 3: Captions, Styles and Timing

In This Module You Will Learn About:

- Text Captions, page 46
- Caption Styles, page 55
- The Timeline, page 59

And You Will Learn To:

- Duplicate a Slide and Hide the Mouse, page 46
- Insert, Resize and Move Text Captions, page 48
- Modify Text Caption Properties, page 51
- Edit the Default Caption Style, page 55
- Reset an Object Style, page 57
- Change an Object's Position & Size, page 58
- View the Timeline, page 59
- Change a Slide's Display Time, page 60
- Use the Timeline to Set Object Display Times, page 61
- Show/Hide Timeline Objects, page 62
- Use the Properties Panel to Control Timing, page 63
- Set Mouse Properties, page 66
- Check Spelling, page 67
- Align Slide Objects, page 69

Text Captions

One of the secrets to successful projects is grabbing the user's attention. Text Captions can prove useful in this regard. You use Text Captions to explain elements that a user sees on-screen. You can have multiple captions on the same slide, and you can control the order in which they appear using the Timeline.

Student Activity: Duplicate a Slide and Hide the Mouse

1. Open a project.

   ☐ using Captivate 5, choose **File > Open**

   ☐ from the Captivate5EssentialsData folder, open **CaptionMe.cptx**

   The project opens using the Workspace you created during the activity on page 13. At this point it really doesn't matter which Workspace you are using (although the one you created is probably a bit less cluttered than some of the others). Unless instructed to do so to support upcoming lessons, please feel free to use any Workspace you like.

2. Preview the lesson.

   ☐ choose **File > Preview > Project**

   This project is demonstrating the process of creating a new folder within a window. The process is similar on most Macs and PCs. The lesson is simple... it shows a mouse moving around the screen and a folder being created. But there is no text (Text Captions) telling a new computer user the importance of folders or explaining what's happening in the lesson. Your goal during the lessons that follow in this module will be to add Text Captions as appropriate.

   ☐ close the Preview

   There are seven slides in the project. You can always tell the slide count by observing the top of the Captivate window (where you can see, among other things, the number of slides in the project).

3. Select Slide 1.

   ☐ using the Filmstrip, select the first slide

   On Slide 1, notice that there is a mouse cursor [cursor icon]. In addition, if you look in the upper left of the slide you will see four red dots in the shape of a box. The four dots indicate where the mouse will appear when the slide plays. There is a blue line curving from the red box toward the mouse. The blue line indicates the path the mouse will take when it ends up over the File menu.

It would be nice to be able to keep the background you see on the slide, lose the mouse and add some text that explains the concept of new folders. After that, the mouse can reappear, but it would be distracting to have it there right now. In the next few steps, you will duplicate the slide; then you will hide the mouse pointer on the duplicate slide.

4. Duplicate a slide.

❐ ensure that **Slide 1** is selected on the Filmstrip

❐ choose **Edit > Duplicate**

Slides 1 and 2 are identical. Your project now contains 8 slides.

5. Hide the mouse pointer on Slide 1.

❐ select **Slide 1** on the Filmstrip

❐ choose **Modify > Mouse > Show Mouse** (to turn the command off)

The mouse pointer disappears from Slide 1. If you were to go to Slide 2, you would notice that the mouse pointer, the red box and pointer path are all there.

Also notice the lower right of the slide thumbnails on the Filmstrip. Slide 1 does not have a mouse icon ; Slide 2 does.

At left, the first slide does not have a mouse cursor on the slide.

6. Save your work.

Student Activity: Insert, Resize and Move Text Captions

1. The CaptionMe project you opened on page 46 should still be open.

2. Restore Object Defaults.

   ☐ choose **Edit** (Mac users, choose **Adobe Captivate**) > **Preferences**

   ☐ from the **Global** Category, select **Defaults**

   ☐ from the **Object Defaults** area, click the **Restore All** button

   Any objects you add to your Captivate projects will now use settings specified by Adobe when Captivate 5 was first installed on your computer. You will learn how to change the Properties of selected objects as you move through lessons in this book.

   ☐ click the **OK** button

3. Insert a Text Caption.

   ☐ go to **Slide 1**

   Currently there are no Text Captions on any slide.

   ☐ choose **Insert > Standard Objects > Text Caption**

   The new Text Caption appears in the middle of your slide.

   ☐ type **New folders can be created in any window** into the new caption

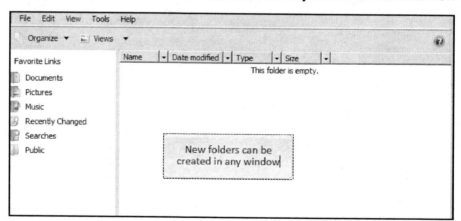

4. Deselect the caption.

   ☐ click in the gray space to the left or right of your slide (the gray space is known as the **Pasteboard**) to deselect the Text Caption

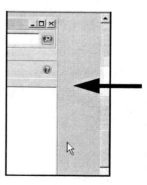

Clicking the Pasteboard is a great way to deselect slide objects. It's located outside of your slide (you may need to zoom out before you can see the Pasteboard).

5. Show the Properties panel for the Text Caption.

   ❏ double-click the Text Caption you just added

The Properties panel opens at the right side of the Captivate window.

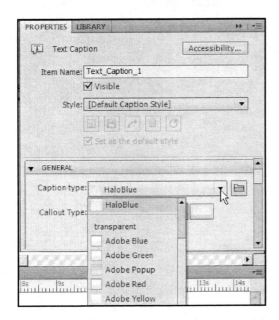

   ❏ scroll down the Properties panel as necessary until you can see the General group

   ❏ from the **Caption type** drop-down menu, select **HaloGreen**

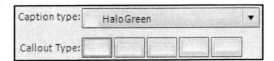

6. Resize a Text Caption.

   ❏ on Slide 1, click one time on the Text Caption

   ❏ position your pointer on one of the Text Caption's resizing squares

   ❏ drag the resizing handle until the size of the Text Caption looks good to you

While the exact size of any Text Caption is always up to you, consider making your Text Captions more **narrow** and **tall** as opposed to wide and short. In my experience, narrow and tall text captions are easier to read than wide and short captions.

7. Reposition a Text Caption.

☐ click once on the **Text Caption**

☐ drag the middle of the caption toward the **left** side of the slide and position it so your slide looks similar to the picture below

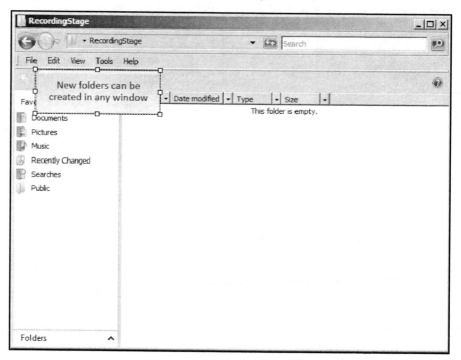

8. Save your work.

Student Activity: Modify Text Caption Properties

1. The CaptionMe project should still be open.

2. Change the size of the Properties panel.

   ☐ on Slide 1, double-click the Text Caption to display the **Properties** panel

   ☐ drag the bottom border of the Properties panel **down** so you can see both the **General** and **Character** groups on the panel

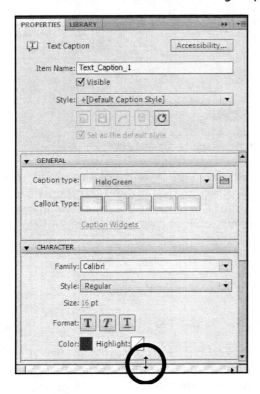

3. Change the Caption type.

   ☐ from the **Caption type** drop-down menu of the General group, select **Adobe Red**

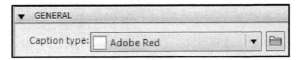

Hey! Did the size of that pesky Text Caption change when you changed the Caption type? You're not seeing things... there's a very good chance that it did. Why? By default, Captivate's **Autosize Captions** feature is enabled. While the feature might seem like a good thing, I've found that it often forces me to do extra work since Text Captions that I've already resized to meet my needs will *magically* resize.

4. Disable the Autosize Captions option.

❏ choose **Edit** (or **Adobe Captivate** if you're on a Mac) **> Preferences**

❏ select the **Global > Defaults** category

❏ from the General area at the bottom of the dialog box, deselect **Autosize Captions**

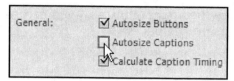

❏ click the **OK** button

5. Resize the Text Caption as you see fit.

6. Change the Caption type from **Adobe Red** to **Frosted**.

While the general appearance of the Text Caption certainly changes, there are no changes to the size of the Text Caption. Is that a good thing or a bad thing? I guess it depends on your perspective. Certainly if you want Captivate to resize your Text Captions moving forward, feel free to turn the option back on.

7. Click on the Pasteboard to deselect the Text Caption.

8. Observe two selection techniques.

❏ on Slide 1, double-click the **middle** of the Text Caption

There are actually two things you should notice as a result of your double-click. First, the **Properties** panel appears at the right side of the window. Given the fact that you have already used the panel a few times, its appearance was probably expected. However, less obvious, there is now a blinking insertion point in the text. You could now edit the text as you would in any text editor.

❏ click on the Pasteboard to deselect the Text Caption

❏ on Slide 1, double-click the **edge** of the Text Caption

The Properties panel appears again. However, this time there is no blinking insertion point in the text and there are resizing handles surrounding the caption. The difference between the two double-clicks is subtle but important. When you double-click the edge of a caption, you'll be able to change the text formatting within the caption without the additional need to select the text. But when you double-click the middle of a caption, you'll enter text editing mode. You'll be able to edit your text, but if you want to change the appearance of the text, you'll need to select the text.

❏ click on the Pasteboard to deselect the caption

9. Change the character formatting for the caption text.

    ❐ on Slide 1, double-click the **corner** of the Text Caption to display the **Properties** panel

    ❐ from the **Character** group, change the font Family to **Verdana**

    ❐ change the Size to **15 pt**

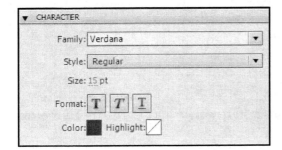

As mentioned on the previous page, you were able to change the font and font size without physically selecting the caption's text.

10. Change the text format.

    ❐ scroll down the Properties panel to the Format group

    ❐ from the Align area, select both **Align Center** (if necessary) and **Align Middle** (if necessary)

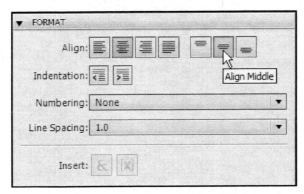

Your Text Caption should look similar to the picture below.

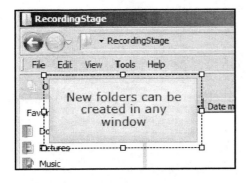

11. Save your work.

Confidence Check

1. The CaptionMe project should still be open.

2. On Slide 1, change the Caption type for the Text Caption to **Adobe Blue**.

3. Choose **Window > Object Toolbar** (to turn the command on, if necessary).

   The Object toolbar typically appears at the far left of your window. Using the Object toolbar, you can add several things on your slide—including Text Captions.

4. Use the **Insert Text Caption** tool on the Object toolbar to insert a second Text Caption with the words **You can give your folder any name up to 255 characters**.

5. Move the new text caption to a new location on your slide.

6. Insert a third Text Caption with the words **Empty folders do not take up disk space--you can have as many folders as you need**.

7. Select your two new captions (you can click on the first one and [shift] click the second one to select both of them).

8. Double-click the edge of either selected caption to display the **Properties** panel.

9. Change the Caption Type to **Frosted**.

10. Using the Properties panel, change the font Family to **Verdana** and the font Size to **15**.

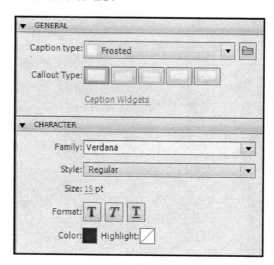

11. Using the Properties panel, ensure that the text is aligned in the **Center** and **Middle**.

12. Save your work.

13. Close the project.

Caption Styles

During the activity that began on page 48, you learned how to insert a Text Caption, and then how to change its formatting. Did you notice that every time you inserted a Text Caption, the appearance of the caption always reverted back to a specific Caption type, font and font size? While it was easy enough to change the appearance of the caption, you will quickly tire of the effort required to change every caption. Instead, you can alter the way Text Captions will appear in this project via Caption Styles. Once you set up the appearance of the Caption Style, any new captions will take on the attributes of the style and save you a ton of manual formatting.

Student Activity: Edit the Default Caption Style

1. Using Captivate, open **TimeMe.cptx** from the Captivate5EssentialsData folder.

   On Slide 1, notice that there are already three Text Captions. Each caption is formatted using the Frosted Caption type. The font Family is Verdana and the size is 15pt.

2. Insert a Text Caption.

   ❏ choose **Insert > Standard Objects > Text Caption** (or click the Insert Text Caption tool on the Object toolbar)

   Notice that the new Text Caption is formatted using a different Caption Type, font and font size.

3. Delete the Text Caption.

   ❏ deselect the caption

   ❏ reselect the caption

   ❏ choose **Edit > Delete**

   You will be asked to confirm the deletion.

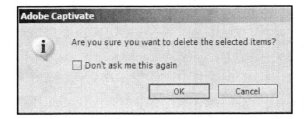

   ❏ click the **OK** button

4. Edit the Default Caption Style.

   ❏ choose **Edit > Object Style Manager**

   ❏ from the top of the Object Style Manager dialog box, select **Default Caption Style**

   ❏ from the Caption group at the right, change the Caption type to **Frosted**

   ❏ from the Character group, change the Family to **Verdana**

☐ change the Size to **15**

☐ from the Format group, ensure that the text is aligned in the **Center** and **Middle**

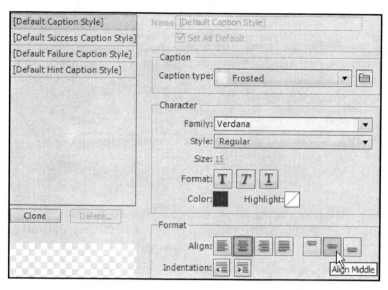

☐ click the **OK** button

5. Insert a Text Caption.

☐ choose **Insert > Standard Objects > Text Caption**

Check it out, this new caption is following the Caption type and formatting you specified in the Object Style Manager. Cool!

☐ type **During this demonstration you will see how to create a new folder** into the new Text Caption

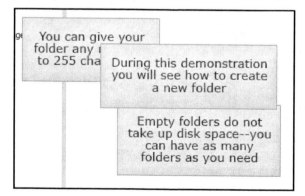

Student Activity: Reset an Object Style

1. The **TimeMe.cptx** project should still be open.

2. Apply different formats to a caption.

   ☐ on Slide 1, double-click the edge of any Text Caption on the slide to display the Properties panel

   ☐ select any Caption type you like

   ☐ double-click the edge of another Text Caption on the slide and select any Caption type you like

   ☐ double-click the edge of a third Text Caption on the slide and select any Caption type you like

   Congratulations, you've got a mess. While one of your captions might be following the default caption style, the others are not. Fortunately, ensuring that the captions match the format you set up in the default caption style is just a click away.

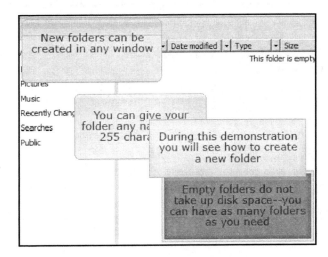

3. Reset the style.

   ☐ select all of the captions on the slide

   ☐ show the **Properties** panel

   ☐ at the top of the Properties panel, click the **Reset Style** button

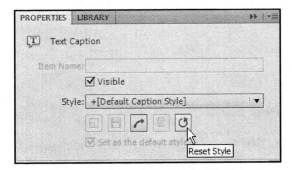

And Bam! All of the captions are following the formatting you specified in the style!

Student Activity: Change an Object's Position & Size

1. Control the slide position and size of a caption.

   ❑ double-click the edge of the caption containing the words "During this demonstration..." to display the Properties panel

   ❑ from the bottom of the Properties panel, click the triangle to the left of the Position & Size group to expand the group

   ❑ change the X value to **42** and the Y value to **150**

   ❑ remove the check mark from **Constrain proportions**

   ❑ change the W to **231** and the H to **90**

Note: If you hadn't turned off the Constrain proportions tool, you would have had a very hard time trying to match the W (Width) and H (Height) values shown at the right because one value would have changed proportionally as you changed the other.

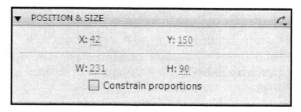

Your slide should look like this:

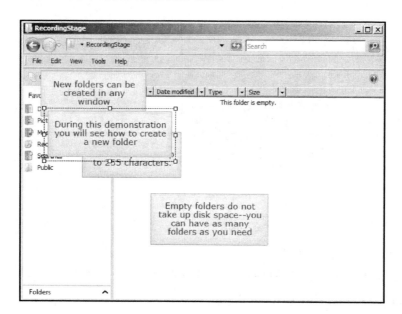

2. Save your work.

3. Preview the slide.

   ❑ choose **File > Preview > Play Slide**

Some of the captions appear at the same time and then disappear... the timing is a mess. Next, you will learn how to use the Timeline to control when the captions appear on the slide, and how long they stay.

The Timeline

The Timeline typically appears at the bottom of the Captivate window (but it can be dragged to different window positions). Each slide has its own unique Timeline. You can use the Timeline to control the timing of any slide object. For instance, using the Timeline, you can force the captions to appear on the slide at the same time, or you can force one caption to appear as another goes away. The Timeline consists of the following features: Object Bars, a Header, a Playhead and Playback Controls. The objects on a project slide are displayed as stacked bars on the left side of the Timeline. The Header at the top of the Timeline indicates time in seconds (and parts of seconds). The Playhead shows the point in time in which the slide is being viewed.

Student Activity: View the Timeline

1. The TimeMe project should still be open and you should still be on Slide 1.

2. View and hide the Timeline.

   ❒ choose **Window > Timeline**

   The Timeline appears just below the slide (it's shown circled in the picture below). However, if the Timeline was already showing on your screen, you've just hidden it (in that case, choose **Window > Timeline** again to show the Timeline).

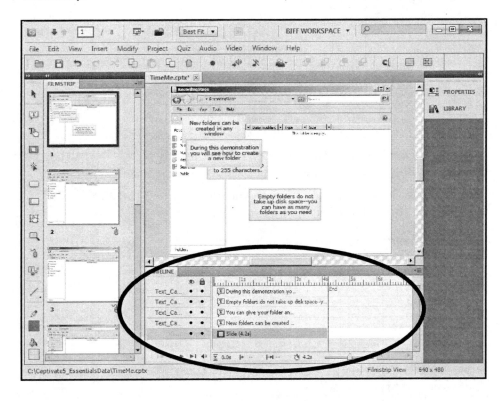

3. The last object on the Timeline is an object that says Slide (4.2s).
   If necessary, resize the Timeline so it is tall enough to see all of the Timeline objects.

Student Activity: Change a Slide's Display Time

1. You should still be on Slide 1 of TimeMe.cptx.

2. Use the Timeline to extend the slide timing to 11 seconds.

   ☐ on the Timeline, position your mouse pointer on the far right edge of the **Slide object** until your mouse pointer looks like a double-headed arrow

   ☐ drag the **right edge** of the object to the **right** until you get to **11** seconds on the Timeline (the word **End** should line up with 11s on the Timeline)

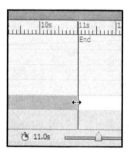

3. Extend slide timing using the Slide Properties.

   ☐ on the Timeline, **double-click** the Slide object to display the Properties panel

   ☐ from the General group, change the slide's Display Time to **20** seconds

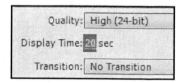

   On the Timeline, you can scroll right and confirm the word **End** lines up with 20s.

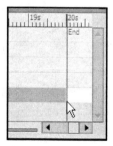

4. Save your work.

Student Activity: Use the Timeline to Set Object Display Times

1. You should still be on Slide 1 of the TimeMe project.

2. Use the Timeline to extend the display time for a Text Caption.

   ❏ on the Timeline, select the object **"During this demonstration..."**

   This object represents the **During this demonstration** Text Caption.

   ❏ on the Timeline, drag the **right edge** of the **"During this demonstration..."** object **right** until the object ends at **5** seconds

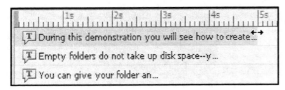

3. Use the Timeline to change when a Text Caption appears on the slide.

   ❏ on the Timeline, select the object **"New folders can be..."**

   ❏ drag the middle of the object **right** and position its left edge at **5** seconds on the Timeline

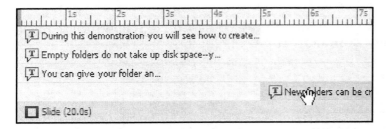

4. Use the Timeline to extend the display time for a Text Caption.

   ❏ on the Timeline, drag the **right edge** of the **"New folders can be..."** object right until the object ends at **10** seconds

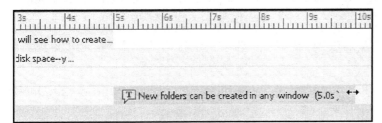

Student Activity: Show/Hide Timeline Objects

1. You should still be on Slide 1 of TimeMe.cptx.

2. Show/Hide all Timeline objects.

   ☐ find the **Show/Hide All Items** button on the upper left of the Timeline

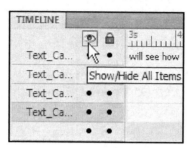

   ☐ click the **Show/Hide All Items** button 👁

   All of the slide objects are hidden.

   ☐ click the **Show/Hide All Items** button 👁 again

   All of the slide objects are back.

3. Hide specific slide objects.

   ☐ click the **circle** (under the **Show/Hide All Items** button) to the left of the **"During this demonstration..."** object

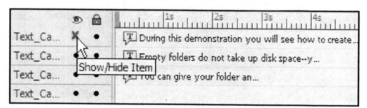

   This time just the specific Text Caption is hidden (there is a large X where the circle once was). The ability to Show/Hide slide objects will prove helpful if you have several objects on the slide and they get in the way of each other.

   ☐ click the **circle** (under the eye) to the left of the **"New folders can be..."** object

   Two of the four slide objects are now hidden. Keep both objects hidden for the next activity.

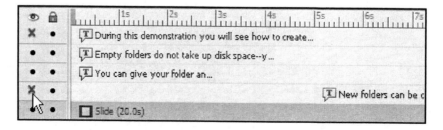

Student Activity: Use the Properties Panel to Control Timing

1. You should still be on Slide 1 of TimeMe.cptx.

2. Use the Properties panel to control Timing.

   ❑ on the Timeline, double-click the "**You can give...**" object to open the Properties panel

   ❑ on the Properties panel, expand the **Timing** group

   ❑ from the **Display For** drop-down menu, ensure **specific time** is selected

   ❑ to the right of **specific time**, change the timing to **5** sec

   ❑ change the **Appear After** timing to **10** sec

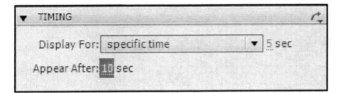

Your Timeline should look like the picture at the right.

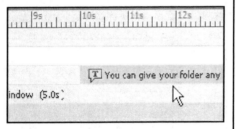

In a moment, you will set it up so that the last Text Caption that will appear on the slide is the **"Empty folders do not..."** caption. Even though that caption will appear last, it is currently in the second vertical position on the Timeline. The vertical position of objects on the Timeline has no bearing on when objects appear on the slide—it is the horizontal position of Timeline objects that controls when objects appear. The caption **"New folders can..."** is in the fourth position on the Timeline even though it will be the second object to appear on the slide. You could easily drag Timeline objects up or down to change their vertical position, but keep in mind that only an object's horizontal Timeline position dictates when an object appears on the slide.

3. Change the stacking order of Timeline objects.

   ❑ use the **Show/Hide** button on the Timeline to show all of the slide objects

   ❑ on the Timeline, drag the **"New folders can..."** object up into the second position on the Timeline

   ❑ drag the **"Empty folders do not..."** object into the fourth vertical position

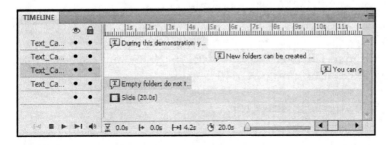

Confidence Check

1. Looking to move closer or farther away from the Timeline? No problem. At the bottom of the Timeline, drag the Zoom slider left or right and notice how doing so changes how close you are to the Timeline.

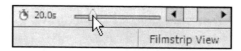

It's up to you to set the zoom percentage to a zoom that is most comfortable to you.

2. Still on Slide 1, set the timing for the **"Empty folders do not..."** Text Caption to the following:

Display for specific time: **5** seconds

Appear after: **15** seconds

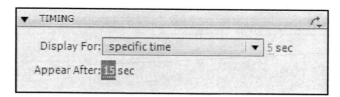

3. Find the **Play** button at the bottom left of the Timeline.

Based on the horizontal position of the Timeline objects, each Text Caption should appear on the slide, one at a time, in 5-second increments. The entire slide should play for 20 seconds.

As the slide plays, notice that a red rectangle moves across the top of the Timeline. The rectangle is known as the **Playhead**. You can drag the Playhead left and right to see how slide objects appear on the slide in relationship to other objects.

4. Drag the Playhead left and right on the Timeline (this is often referred to as "scrubbing the Timeline") and notice how objects on the slide change depending on the Playhead position.

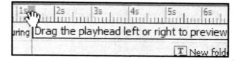

5. Go to **Slide 2** and insert a Text Caption with the following text (you learned how to insert a Text Caption on page 48):

Watch as the File menu is selected

6. Show the Properties of the new Text Caption and, from the General group, change its **Callout Type** to the third type from the left.

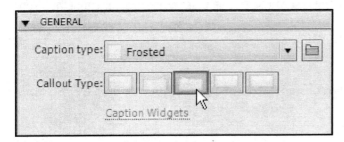

7. Resize and move the Text Caption so that its position is similar to the picture below.

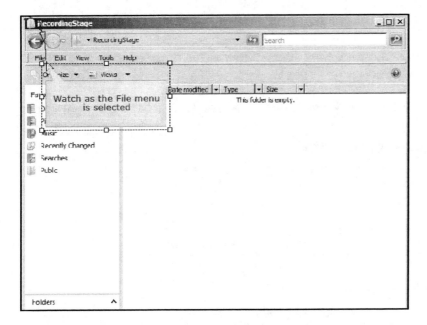

8. Use the **Play** button on the Timeline to play the slide.

   The Text Caption should appear right away. However, the mouse pointer appears on the slide a bit too soon and takes too long to get to the File menu. You will fix both problems next when you set the Mouse properties.

9. Save and close the project.

Student Activity: Set Mouse Properties

1. Open **MouseMeSpellMe.cptx** from the Captivate5EssentialsData folder.

2. Show the Mouse properties.

   ☐ go to Slide 2

   ☐ on the Timeline, double-click the **Mouse** object to display the Mouse properties

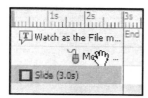

3. Set the Mouse Display time and Appear after properties.

   ☐ expand the **Timing** group

   ☐ change the **Display For** time to **1.6** sec (the field to the right of Display for specific time)

   ☐ change the **Appear After** time to **3** sec

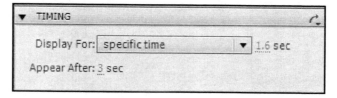

   The Timeline should look like this:

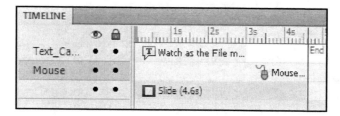

4. **Play** the slide.

   Notice the improved timing between the caption and the mouse.

Student Activity: Check Spelling

1. The MouseMeSpellMe.cptx project should still be open.

2. Disable Calculate Caption Timing.

   ❒ choose **Edit** (or **Adobe Captivate** if you are using a Mac) **> Preferences**

   ❒ from the **Global** Category, select **Defaults**

   ❒ from the General area, deselect **Calculate Caption Timing** (there should not be a check mark next to the option)

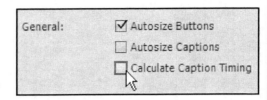

Depending on how you look at the world, the Calculate Caption Timing feature is one of those "glass half empty, half full" kind of commands. With the option selected, Captivate will automatically calculate how long a caption will stay on a slide based on the number of characters contained in the caption. *That's a glass half-full kind of thing—you don't have to worry about the timing.*

However, if you select a specific display time (as you have done with the captions in this project) and then change a caption's content, you would inadvertently reset your specified time to Captivate's calculated caption timing. *That's a glass half-empty kind of thing—you'll have to reset the timing via the Timeline or through the Text Caption's properties.* Personally, I'm not a fan of Calculate Caption Timing and *always* disable the option.

   ❒ click the **OK** button

3. On **Slide 1**, notice that there are typos in the Text Captions (from misspelled words to double words).

4. Spell check the project.

   ❒ choose **Project > Check Spelling**

   The first word that is flagged as mispelled is **foolders**.

   ❒ ensure that **folders** is selected in the **Suggestions** area

   ❒ click the **Change** button

   The next error is the double word.

   ❒ click the **Delete** button

The word "demmonstratoin" is flagged.

❏ select **demonstration** from the list of Suggestions

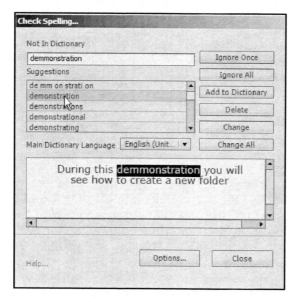

❏ click the **Change** button

The word "selectid" is flagged.

❏ select **selected** from the list of Suggestions

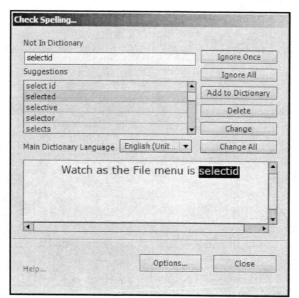

❏ click the **Change** button

❏ click the **OK** button

5. Save your work.

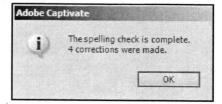

Student Activity: Align Slide Objects

1. The MouseMeSpellMe.cptx project should still be open.

2. Go to Slide 1.

   ❏ hide the first Text Caption, **During this demonstration...** (you learned how to hide slide objects on page 62)

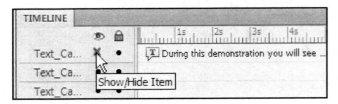

3. View the Alignment toolbar.

   ❏ choose **Window > Align**

   The Alignment toolbar should appear at the top of your window. If you use your mouse to point at each of the tools, you'll see a Tooltip that will tell you what the tool does.

4. Select multiple captions.

   ❏ click one time on the caption containing "New folders can be..."

   ❏ press and hold the [**shift**] key

   ❏ click one time on the caption containing "You can give your folder..."

   ❏ keep the [**shift**] down

   ❏ click one time on the caption containing "Empty folders do not take..."

   ❏ release the [**shift**] key

5. Left-align the selected captions.

   ❏ on the **Alignment** toolbar, click the **Align Left** tool

   ❏ on the **Alignment** toolbar, click the **Distribute Vertically** tool

   The captions are now lined up with the first caption you selected (objects with white handles serve as anchors and other selected objects move to the anchors when you align objects). In addition, the vertical space between the captions vertically is now perfect.

Confidence Check

1. The MouseMeSpellMe.cptx project should still be open.

2. Ensure you are on Slide 1 and choose **File > Preview > Next 5 slides**.

3. As Slide 1 plays, notice that the timing of the Text Captions is pretty good. But don't you think it would be better if the three Text Captions (after the first one) stayed around for the duration of the slide? Sure you do!

4. Close the preview and return to Slide 1.

5. Select all three of the Text Captions on Slide 1 (the first Text Caption should still be hidden).

6. Right-click any of the selected Text Captions and choose **Show for rest of the slide**.

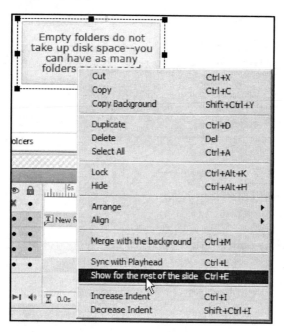

On the Timeline, notice that the selected objects have stretched to the end of the slide.

7. Preview the next five slides now and notice that after the first Text Caption goes away, the remaining captions show for the rest of the slide.

8. Close the preview.

9. Save your work.

Bonus Confidence Check

1. The MouseMeSpellMe.cptx project should still be open.

2. Choose **File > Save As** and rename the file **MyCaptionLab**. (Ensure you are saving to the Captivate5EssentialsData folder.)

3. Go to **Slide 4** and add a Text Caption that says: **Watch as the New command is selected**.

4. Ensure that the **Callout Type** is set to the third one and position it on the slide as shown below.

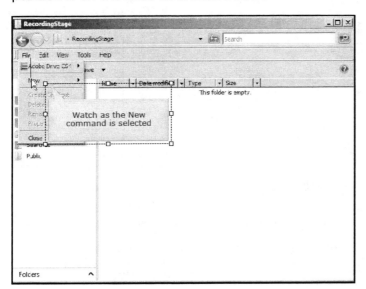

5. Adjust the timing of the slide objects to suit your taste.

6. Go to **Slide 5** and add a Text Caption that says: **Watch as the Folder command is selected**

7. Change the Callout Type to the third one and position the caption on the slide as shown below.

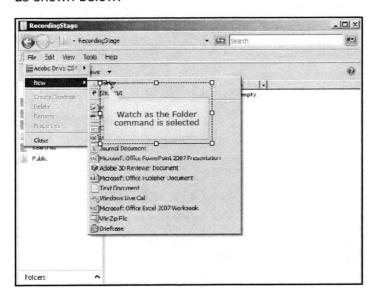

8. Adjust the timing of the slide objects to suit your taste.

9. Go to **Slide 7** and add a Text Caption that says: **Watch as the new Folder is selected**

10. Change the Callout Type to the third one and position the caption on the slide as shown in the picture below.

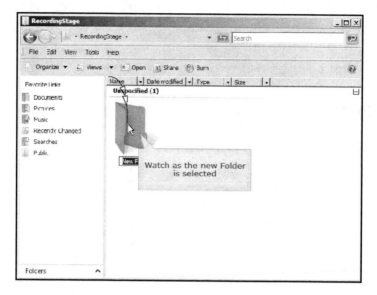

11. Adjust the timing of the slide objects to suit your taste.

12. Preview the project **In Web Browser**. (File > Preview)

13. When finished, close the browser and return to Captivate.

14. If necessary, go through your slides and adjust object and slide timings to suit your taste.

15. Preview the project **In Web Browser**.

16. When finished, close the browser.

17. Save and close the project.

iCONLOGiC
"Skills and Drills" Learning

Module 4: Images and Drawing Objects

In This Module You Will Learn About:

- Slide Quality, page 74
- Blank Slides, page 75
- Images, page 76
- The Library, page 79
- Image Editing, page 83
- Mouse Visuals and Sounds, page 90
- Drawing Objects, page 92

And You Will Learn To:

- Change Slide Background Quality, page 74
- Insert and Delete Slides, page 75
- Insert an Image, page 76
- Set Image Size and Slide Position, page 78
- Use the Library, page 79
- Manage Unused Project Assets, page 82
- Crop an Image, page 83
- Create an Image Watermark, page 85
- Work With Image Stacks, page 88
- Add a Visual Click and Sound, page 90
- Draw a Line, page 92

Slide Quality

You can easily change the quality level for any slide background. There are four quality options: Low (8-bit), Optimized, JPEG and High (24-bit). If you are not sure of the option to choose, consider Optimized or JPEG.

> **Note:** Selecting Optimized, JPEG or the High Quality format will likely increase the size of your published lesson.

Student Activity: Change Slide Background Quality

1. Using Captivate 5, open **ImageMe** from the Captivate5EssentialsData folder.

    This project contains eight slides. Most of the slides have at least one Text Caption (you learned how to insert captions beginning on page 48). There are no images except for the slides themselves (the slide backgrounds).

    Notice the slide backgrounds. Each background contains a blue title bar that includes a blend of color that goes from dark blue to light blue.

2. Preview the project.

    As you watch the Preview, notice that the title bar's color blend simply does not look all that good. Instead of a gradual color blend from the dark blue to the lighter blue, you can actually see vertical bands of colors.

3. Close the Preview.

4. Improve the slide background Quality.

    ☐ using the Filmstrip, select all of the slides (you can select the first slide, press [**Shift**] on your keyboard and then click the last slide to select them all)

    ☐ choose **Window > Properties** to open the Properties panel

    ☐ from the General group, **Quality** drop-down menu, select **High (24-bit)**

5. Preview the project.

    You should be able to notice that the color quality is much improved.

6. Save your work.

Blank Slides

In the next activity, you will learn how to add, delete and move Blank slides. Blank slides are handy for adding Title slides (also known as Splash Screen) and Ending slides to your project.

Student Activity: Insert and Delete Slides

1. The ImageMe.cptx project should still be open.

2. Insert a Blank slide.

   ☐ select the first slide

   ☐ choose **Insert > Blank Slide**

   A new slide is created and opened. Your new slide appears after the selected first slide.

3. Delete a slide.

   ☐ on the Filmstrip, select the new slide (Slide 2) and choose **Edit > Delete**

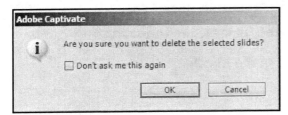

   ☐ click the **OK** button to confirm the deletion

4. Insert another Blank slide.

   ☐ select the **first slide** again and then choose **Insert > Blank Slide**

5. Reposition the new slide.

   ☐ on the Filmstrip, drag the new slide above Slide 1

6. Save your work.

Images

Captivate lets you import myriad graphic formats onto a slide including, but not limited to, native **Photoshop** documents (PSDs), **BMPs** (Windows Bitmap), **GIFs** (Graphics Interchange Format), **JPG** or **JPEG** (Joint Photographic Expert Group), **ICOs** (icons), **WMFs** (MetaFiles), **EMFs** (Enhanced MetaFiles), **PNGs** (Portable Network Graphics) and **POTs** (PowerPoint Templates).

Once the image has been imported, you can resize it, crop it and apply multiple effects to it.

Student Activity: Insert an Image

1. The ImageMe.cptx project should still be open.

2. Insert an image onto Slide 1.

   ☐ go to **Slide 1**

   ☐ choose **Insert > Image** (careful, there is a similar command in the Insert menu called Image Slide... you're looking for the **Image** command which is near the bottom of the menu)

   ☐ navigate to the **Captivate5EssentialsData** folder

   ☐ from the **images_animation** folder, open **logo.gif**

   The image should now appear in the middle of Slide 1.

3. Reposition an image.

   ☐ position your mouse in the **center** of the logo

   ☐ drag the logo to the **upper right** of the slide

4. Resize an image manually.

    ❏ position your mouse pointer over the resizing handle in the **lower left** of the image

    ❏ drag the handle down and to the left to make the image much larger

Ouch! Perhaps stretching an image larger isn't such a good idea. Notice that the image pixelates (it gets blurry), which is something that happens when you resize some image formats larger.

5. Reset an image's size.

    ❏ double-click the image to open the Properties panel

    ❏ click the **Reset To Original Size** button

Reset To Original Size

The image should be the same size that it was when you first imported it. It's probably in the middle of your slide as well, which is fine.

6. Save your work.

Student Activity: Set Image Size and Slide Position

1. The ImageMe.cptx project should still be open.

2. Specify a specific image size and slide position.

   ☐ if the Properties panel is no longer on the screen, double-click the logo image on **Slide 1** to reopen it

   ☐ scroll down the Properties panel to the **Position & Size** group

   ☐ expand the group if necessary

   ☐ change both the X and Y values to **36**

   This will force the image to appear 36 pixels from the upper left of the slide. (A pixel is a square and is the smallest part of a digitized object on your computer screen.)

   ☐ change the **Width** to **180**

   Notice that since Constrain Proportions is selected, the Height automatically changes to **66**.

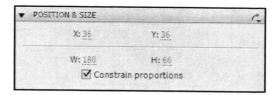

The logo should now be positioned in the upper left of the first slide and it's a bit smaller.

3. Save your work.

The Library

Your slides can contain audio, background images, images, animations, linked PowerPoint presentations and more. Those assets are monitored by Captivate's Library panel (available via the Window menu). Once the Library is opened, you can add previously imported assets onto any slide by simply dragging the object's name from the Library and onto the slide.

Student Activity: Use the Library

1. The ImageMe.cptx project should still be open.

2. Show the Library.

   ☐ choose **Window > Library**

   The Library panel appears at the far right of your window. More likely than not, the Library is a bit too small to see the assets it contains.

   ☐ stretch the Library panels until the Library is sized similarly to the image below

3. Use the library to add an image to a slide.

   ☐ go to **Slide 2**

   ☐ from the Library panel, open the **Images** folder, if necessary, to display the images currently in the project

   ☐ on the Library's Images folder, click once on **logo.gif**

At the top of the Library, notice that you can see a preview of the selected image.

❐ drag **logo.gif** from the Library panel and onto Slide 2

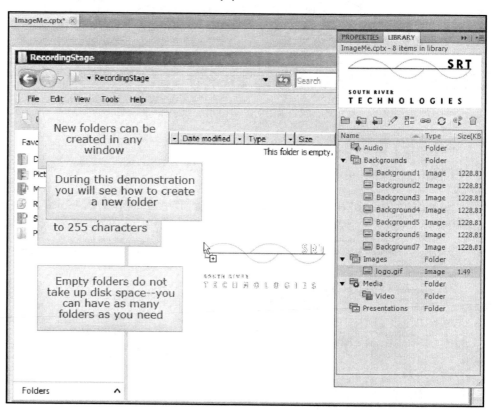

The logo appears on Slide 2. The information in the Library could prove helpful. Notice that the logo.gif row contains information such as the size of the image and how many times the image has been used in the project (you may have to stretch the Library panel wider to see the Use Count column).

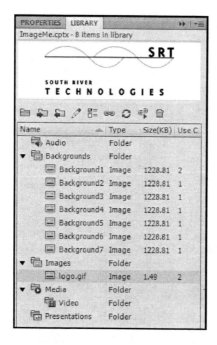

4. View specific image usage.

❒ at the top of the Library, click the **Usage** button

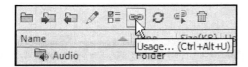

A dialog box appears, telling you exactly which two slides are using the image.

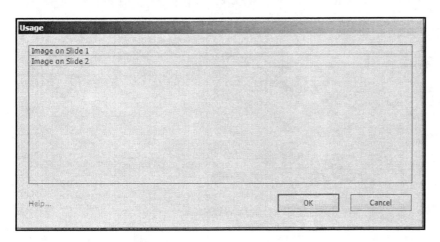

❒ click the **OK** button

Note: You can open Libraries from any Captivate project by clicking the Open Library button on the Library and opening any project. The assets used in the other Captivate project will appear on the Library panel and you can add them to the current project.

Student Activity: Manage Unused Project Assets

1. The ImageMe.cptx project should still be open.

2. Insert an image.

   ☐ go to the last slide in the project and choose **Insert > Image**

   ☐ from the **images_animation folder**, open **beachBunny.jpg**

   The image should now appear on the slide and should still be selected.

3. Delete the image.

   ☐ select the beachBunny image you just imported and choose **Edit > Delete**

   ☐ click **OK** to confirm the deletion

   Display the Library panel (Window menu) and notice that the image you deleted is still listed, even though it is no longer used in the project. It's a good idea to routinely remove unused assets from your project (which will lower the size of your project).

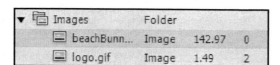

4. Delete unused items.

   ☐ from the top of the Library, click the **Select Unused Items** button

   ☐ from the top of the Library, click the **Delete** button 🗑

   ☐ click **OK** to confirm the deletion

5. Delete the image from Slide 2.

   ☐ go to Slide 2

   ☐ select and delete the logo you added to this slide earlier

   The logo is still being used on Slide 1.

Image Editing

While Captivate is not an image editing program like Adobe Photoshop, you can control several aspects of an image including flipping it horizontally and vertically, controlling its rotation, setting its brightness and contrast, and even cropping it. During the next activity you will crop part of the logo image you are using on the first slide.

Student Activity: Crop an Image

1. The ImageMe.cptx project should still be open.

2. Crop an image.

   ❑ go to Slide 1

   ❑ double-click the logo to display the **Properties** panel

   ❑ from the **Image Edit** group on the Properties panel, click the **Crop Image** button 🔲

   The Resize/Crop Image dialog box opens.

   ❑ on the right side of the dialog box, deselect **Constraint Proportion**

   ❑ in the middle of the dialog box, drag the bottom, center resizing handle up just enough to remove the words South River Technologies from the image

   ❑ click the **OK** button

   The words "South River Technologies" have been cropped out of the image.

3. Use the Properties panel to specify a slide position.

   ❑ if the Properties panel is no longer on the screen, double-click the logo image on **Slide 1** to reopen it

   ❑ scroll down the Properties panel to the **Position & Size** group

   ❑ change both the X and Y values to **36**

   The logo should once again be positioned in the upper left of the slide.

4. Copy and paste the logo on Slide 1 to Slide 2.

   ❑ go to Slide 1 and select the logo

   ❑ choose **Edit > Copy**

   ❑ go to Slide 2

   ❑ choose **Edit > Paste**

5. Change the transparency of the logo.

   ❑ double-click the logo on Slide 2 to open the Properties panel

   ❑ from the **Image Edit** group of the Properties panel, change the **Alpha** to **50**

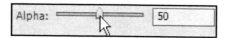

The image appears faded. This is a great technique for creating watermarks out of any image. At 100% Alpha, an image would be opaque. At 0%, the image would be completely transparent and become invisible.

6. Change the slide position of the image.

   ❑ drag the logo **down** and to the bottom **right** of Slide 2

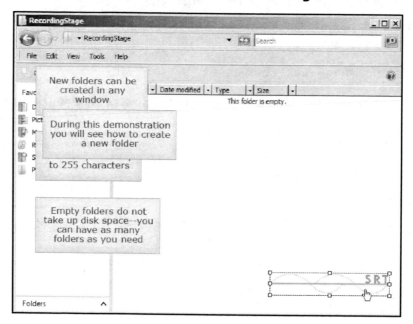

Perhaps you'd like a faded image to appear in the same location on every slide for the rest of the lesson. During the next activity you will learn how.

7. Save your work.

Student Activity: Create an Image Watermark

1. The ImageMe.cptx project should still be open.

2. Show an image for an entire project to create a watermark.

   ❏ double-click the logo on Slide 2 to display the Properties

   ❏ from the **Timing** group of the Properties panel, change the **Display For** to **rest of project**

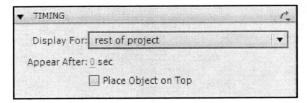

3. Preview the next five slides.

   ❏ ensure you are on Slide 2 and then choose **File > Preview > Next 5 slides**

   As the five slides play, notice that the logo appears in the exact location of every slide.

4. When the preview is finished, close the preview.

Student Activity: Control Image Timing and Transition

1. The ImageMe.cptx project should still be open.

2. Change the Timing for the logo.

   ☐ go to **Slide 1**

   ☐ double-click the **logo**

   ☐ from the **Timing** group of the Properties panel, change the **Display For** to **specific time** and **4** sec

   ☐ change the **Appear After** to **1** sec

3. Change the logo's Transition.

   ☐ from the **Transition** group of the Properties panel, change the **Transition Effect** to **Fade In Only**

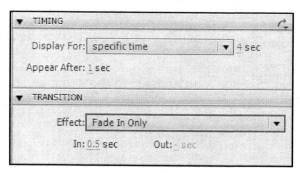

Your Timeline should look like this:

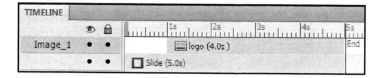

4. Save your work.

5. Preview just the slide.

   ☐ ensure that you are on Slide 1 and then choose **File > Preview > Play Slide**

The logo should fade in after one second. You have also set the image timing to four seconds but since the logo is the only thing on the slide, this change is not obvious.

Confidence Check

1. Insert the following two images onto Slide 1 of the
    ImageMe project:

    SkillsDrills.jpg

    Lesson1.jpg

2. Move the images around the slide until it looks like the
    picture below.

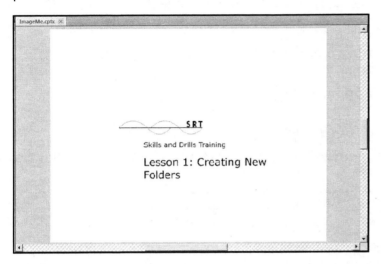

3. Change the Image Properties for the
    SkillsDrills image as follows:

    Display For to **3** sec
    Appear After to **2** sec
    Transition Effect to **Fade In Only**

4. Change the Image Properties for the
    Lesson1 image as follows:

    Display For to **2** sec
    Appear After to **3** sec
    Transition Effect to **Fade In Only**

    The Timeline should look like this:

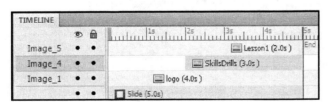

5. Preview the slide.

    You should see each image appear, one after the other.

6. Save your work.

Student Activity: Work With Image Stacks

1. The ImageMe.cptx project should still be open.

2. Insert an image and set timing at the same time.

    ☐ still on Slide 1, choose **Insert > Image**

    ☐ open **mainart** from the images_animation folder

3. Change the display options for the mainart image.

    ☐ double-click the **mainart** image

    ☐ from the **Timing** group of the Properties panel, change the **Display For** to **specific time** to **5** sec

    ☐ change the **Appear After** to **0** sec

4. Change the image's Transition.

    ☐ from the **Transition** group of the Properties panel, change the **Transition Effect** to **Fade In Only**

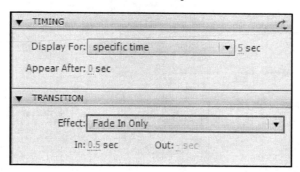

Your Timeline should look like the image below. The mainart image is the same size as the slide (640x480 pixels). It is so big, in fact, that it covers the other images on the slide.

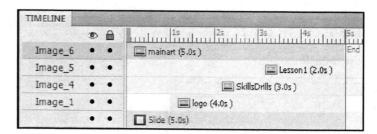

5. Change the order of the image.

    ☐ with the **mainart** selected, choose **Modify > Arrange > Send to Back**

Because you moved the mainart image behind all of the others, you can now see the other slide images.

Confidence Check

1. Move the images until your slide looks similar to the image below.

2. Go to **Slide 4** and make the following changes:

   Change the mouse Display For timing to one-half second. (You learned how to control the mouse Display For timing on page 66.)

   Change the slide Display Time to one-half second. (You learned how to control slide Display Time on page 60.)

3. Go to **Slide 7** and make the following changes:

   Change the mouse Display Time to one-half second.

   Change the slide Display Time to one-half second.

4. Save your work.

5. Preview the project.

   As you watch the demonstration, notice on Slide 1 that the mainart image appears followed by the logo, the skills and drills image and, finally, the Lesson 1 image.

   Because the only action on Slides 4 and 7 is a mouse click, you have made this a more realistic demonstration by speeding up the action on both of these slides.

6. Close the project.

Mouse Visuals and Sounds

If your project is intended to demonstrate a desktop or Web application, including the mouse pointer is a good idea. If you do include the mouse pointer, you can also include a visual mouse click and click sound that will further enhance the user experience.

Student Activity: Add a Visual Click and Sound

1. Open **MouseVisualMe** from the Captivate5EssentialsData folder.

2. Go to Slide 4.

   This is the slide where the mouse has made it to the **File** menu and the menu is clicked. This is a perfect place to add both a visual mouse click and click sound.

3. Add a mouse click sound.

   ❑ on the Timeline for Slide 4, double-click the **mouse** and show its **Properties**

   ❑ from the Captions area, select **Mouse Click Sound**

   ❑ select **Single-click** from the drop-down menu

4. Add a visual mouse click.

   ❑ select **Show Mouse Click**

   ❑ select **Custom** from the drop-down menu

   ❑ select any of the mouse clicks you like from the drop-down menu (you can preview the mouse click visual by clicking the Play button to the right of the selection)

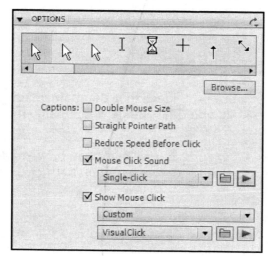

Confidence Check

1. Go to Slide 3 and preview the next five slides.

   When Slide 4 plays, you should see and hear the mouse click.

2. Add a visual mouse click and mouse click sound to the mouse pointer on **Slides 5**, **6** and **8**.

3. Show the Properties of Slide 2 and change the Transition to **Wipe**.

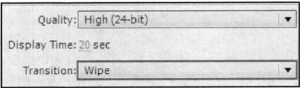

Quality:	High (24-bit)	▼
Display Time:	20 sec	
Transition:	Wipe	▼

4. Save your work.

5. Preview the project.

   As the lesson plays, pay particular attention to the **Wipe** transition you added that will soften the abrupt jump between Slides 1 and 2. In addition, notice the visual mouse clicks and sounds you added.

6. When the preview is finished, close the preview.

7. Keep the project open for the next activity.

Drawing Objects

If you need to create objects such as lines (with arrows), circles, rectangles or complex shapes such as polygons, there is no need to leave Captivate. Using Captivate's Drawing Objects menu, you can quickly add these kinds of objects to a slide.

Student Activity: Draw a Line

1. The **MouseVisualMe** project should still be open.

2. Change a Text Caption's style.

   ☐ go to **Slide 3**

   ☐ drag the Text Caption down approximately 1 inch lower on the slide

   ☐ from the General group on the Properties panel, select the first **Callout Type**

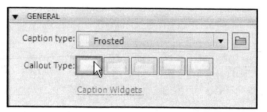

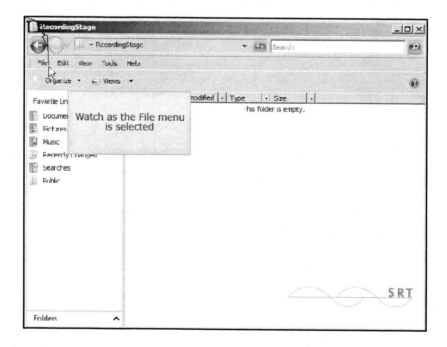

3. Draw a line.

   ☐ on the **Object Toolbar** (which is typically located at the left of the Captivate window), select the **Line Tool**

   ☐ draw a line anywhere on the slide

4. Change the location and size of the line.

☐ double-click the **Line** to display its Properties

☐ on the **Position** group, change the Start Point to **X: 40 Y: 74**

☐ change the End Point to **X:77 Y:122**

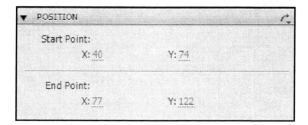

5. Change the Line's width.

☐ on the **Fill & Stroke** group, change the Width to **4**

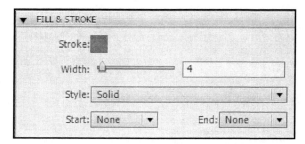

6. Use the Pick Color tool to match a color.

☐ with the Line still selected and still working in the **Fill & Stroke** group of the Properties panel, click the color chip to the right of **Stroke**

☐ from the right side of the colors, select the **Pick Color** tool

☐ using the Pick Color tool, point to the right edge of the Text Caption on the slide

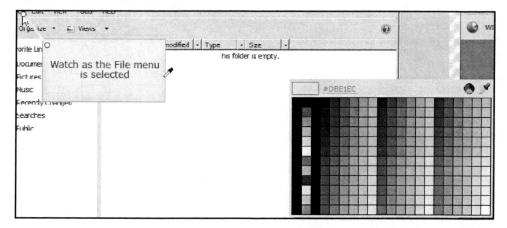

When the Pick Color tool gets to the edge of the Text Caption, the color is absorbed by the Pick Color tool. How cool is that?

☐ click on the **right edge** of the Text Caption to pick up the light blue color

Confidence Check

1. With the Line still selected and still working in the Fill & Stroke group of the Properties panel, select **Arrow** from the Start drop-down menu.

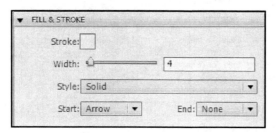

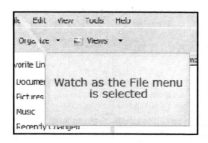

Your Timeline should look like this:

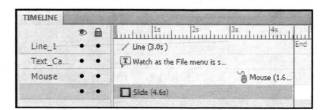

2. Select the Text Caption and bring it in front of the line (Modify menu).

3. Preview the slide and notice that the Text Caption and your arrow appear on the slide at the same time, followed by the mouse cursor.

4. Save and close the project.

iCONLOGiC

"Skills and Drills" Learning

Module 5: Pointers, Buttons and Highlight Boxes

In This Module You Will Learn About:

- Pointer Paths and Types, page 96
- Buttons, page 98
- Highlight Boxes, page 104

And You Will Learn To:

- Modify the Mouse Pointer, page 96
- Edit Slide and Object Display Times, page 98
- Insert a Text Button, page 99
- Set a Button's Timing and Options, page 101
- Work With Image Buttons, page 102
- Insert and Format a Highlight Box, page 104

Pointer Paths and Types

When you record a lesson using Captivate, every move you make with the mouse can be recorded, including menu selections, dialog box selections and the path your mouse takes as you move it around the screen. Captivate includes the ability to easily change the pointer path without having to rerecord your project.

When you record a Demonstration (you learned how on page 29), Captivate only recognizes mouse cursors that are available in the Captivate gallery (a folder within the Captivate application folder where Captivate is installed). If you record an application that contains a cursor Captivate cannot recognize, the pointer will appear as an incorrect cursor or a black box. Luckily, you can change the way the mouse pointer looks on a slide or throughout the project. The pointer can be changed to a variety of icons such as a hand, a vertical resize pointer, or a drag pointer. If you are not happy with the pointer icons that come with Captivate, you can select any system pointer or existing CUR (cursor) file on your hard drive or network as the pointer image.

When you change the pointer type, you will notice two options: Project Pointers and Current Theme Pointers. Project Pointers are resident in the Captivate gallery and are available in any Captivate project. Current Theme Pointers reflect the Windows theme you are currently using. If you change the Windows theme, the choices on this menu change.

Student Activity: Modify the Mouse Pointer

1. Using Captivate 5, open **PointerPathMe** from the Captivate5EssentialsData folder.

2. Hide slide objects.

   ☐ go to Slide 3

   ☐ if necessary, display the Timeline (Window menu)

   ☐ on the Timeline, click the **Show/Hide Item** button to the left of the caption containing the words "Watch as..."

   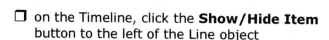

   The caption should now be hidden.

   ☐ on the Timeline, click the **Show/Hide Item** button to the left of the Line object

   The Line should now be hidden. On the slide, notice that the tip of the pointer (the tip of the mouse pointer is called the "hot spot") is pointing just the right of the "e" in "File." It might look a bit better if the hot spot of the mouse pointer was optically centered over the word "File."

3. Edit the pointer path.

   ☐ drag the mouse pointer **up** and to the **left** just a bit so that it is more optically centered over the word **File**

4. Go to Slide 4.

Houston, we have a problem! Notice that the mouse pointer on Slide 4 didn't get the memo from the mouse pointer on Slide 3 (informing it that it needs to move up and to the left). You can get a better look at the problem by switching between Slides 3 and 4 and you'll clearly see the pointer jump between the two slides. Hold on for a bit of magic as you tell the pointer on Slide 4 to match the position of the pointer on Slide 3.

5. Align the slide position of the mouse pointer with the previous slide.

   ❏ still working on Slide 4, select the **Mouse** object on the Timeline

   ❏ choose **Modify > Mouse > Align to Previous Slide**

   Without this wonderful feature, you would have been forced to drag the pointer on Slide 4 a bit at a time, and constantly switch between Slides 3 and 4 to ensure that the alignment was perfect. The Align to feature made quick work of the process.

6. Save your work.

7. Change the pointer type.

   ❏ go to **Slide 9**

   Notice the pointer type is a standard white pointer.

   ❏ on the Timeline, double-click the mouse to display the Properties panel

   ❏ from the Options group at the top of the Properties panel, scroll right and select the **Hand Pointer**

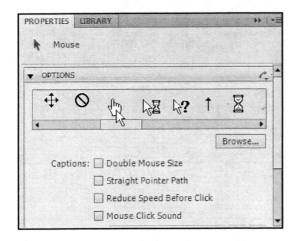

On the slide, the mouse pointer now looks like a Hand Pointer. This change will only affect the pointer on Slide 9.

8. Save your work and close the project.

Buttons

Buttons provide you with an easy way to add interactivity to a slide. There are three types of buttons: Text, Transparent and Image. A Text button can contain any word or phrase you care to type, such as "Continue" or "Begin." You have complete control over the font and font size used in the Text button; however, the larger the font size, the larger the button will be. With a Transparent button, the button cannot contain text, but you can control its Frame and Fill color. With an Image button, you can specify a different image for each button state: Up, Down and Over.

Student Activity: Edit Slide and Object Display Times

1. Open **ButtonHighlightMe** from the Captivate5EssentialsData folder.

2. Increase the slide's Display Time.

    ❑ on Filmstrip, double-click **Slide 1** to display the **Properties** panel

    ❑ change the Display Time to **10** sec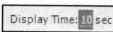

3. Change the Display time for slide object to Rest of slide.

    ❑ on the Timeline, select the **Lesson1** object

    ❑ press [**Shift**] on your keyboard and select the last object (**mainart.jpg**)

    ❑ release [**Shift**]

    All of the slide objects should now be selected.

    ❑ choose **Modify > Show for the rest of the slide**

    Your Timeline should look like this:

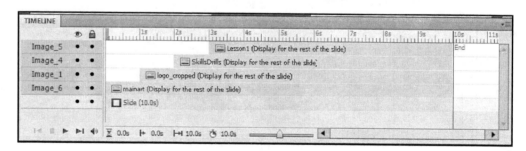

Student Activity: Insert a Text Button

1. ButtonHighlightMe.cp should still be open and you should still be on **Slide 1**.

   You are about to add a button to the slide that will freeze the project on Slide 1 until your learner clicks the button. Once clicked, the button will jump the learner to the next slide in the lesson.

2. Edit the button style for a Text button.

   ☐ choose **Edit > Object Style Manager**

   ☐ at the far left of the dialog box, click the triangle to expand the **Standard Objects** group

   ☐ select **Button**

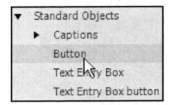

   ☐ from the middle column, select **[Default Text Button Style]**

   ☐ from the Character group at the right, change the font Family to **Verdana**

   ☐ change the Size to **15**

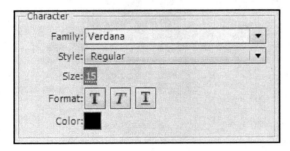

   ☐ ensure that the Color is **black**

   ☐ click the **OK** button

3. Insert a Text button.

   ☐ choose **Insert > Standard Objects > Button**

   The new button appears in the middle of the slide.

4. Save your work.

5. Add a caption to the button.

   ☐ double-click the button to show the Properties panel

   ☐ from the General group, change the Caption to the word **Begin**

6. Set the button's Action.

   ❑ on the Properties panel, scroll down to the **Action** group

   ❑ from the **On Success** drop-down menu, select **Go to the next slide**

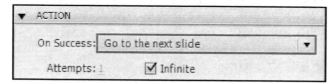

7. Set the button's Timing.

   ❑ on the Properties panel, scroll down to the **Timing** group

   ❑ from the **Display For** drop-down menu, select **rest of slide**

   ❑ ensure that **Appear After** is set to **0 sec**

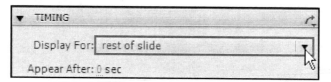

8. Drag the button until its position is similar to the picture below.

9. Save your work.

10. Preview the next 5 slides.

   ❑ press [**F10**] on your keyboard (Mac users, press [**Command**] [**F10**])

As the first slide plays, notice that the action stops too soon—not all of the images have had a chance to appear. You will fix that problem next.

11. Close the preview.

Student Activity: Set a Button's Timing and Options

1. ButtonHighlightMe.cptx should still be open and you should still be on **Slide 1**.

2. Edit the button's Properties so that it pauses after the appropriate time.

   ❒ double-click the button on Slide 1 to display the **Properties** panel

   ❒ from the **Timing** group, change the **Pause after** to **4.5** seconds

   Setting the Pause after to 4.5 seconds will give the other slide objects enough time to appear on the slide before the slide action stops.

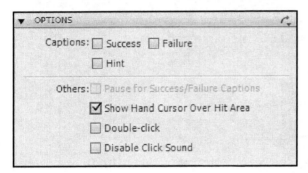

   ❒ from the **Options** group of the Properties panel, select
      Show Hand Cursor Over Hit Area

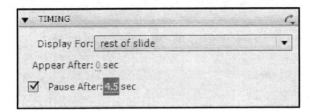

3. Save your work.

4. Preview the next 5 slides.

   After Slide 1 appears, notice that all of the slide elements show up on the slide and then the lesson stops—waiting for you to click the **Begin** button.

5. Position your pointer over the button and notice that your mouse pointer changes to a hand mouse cursor—thanks to the **Show Hand Cursor Over Hit Area** option you selected.

6. Click the button to jump to the next slide in the project.

7. Close the preview.

Student Activity: Work With Image Buttons

1. ButtonHighlightMe.cptx should still be open and you should still be on **Slide 1**.

2. Edit the button style for an Image button.

   ❏ choose **Edit > Object Style Manager**

   ❏ at the far left of the dialog box, click the triangle to expand the **Standard Objects** group

   ❏ select **Button**

   ❏ from the middle column, select **[Default Image Button Style]**

   ❏ from the Button Type menu at the right, scroll down and select **next_bluesquare**

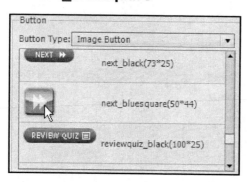

   ❏ click the **OK** button

3. Apply a different style to a button.

   ❏ on Slide 1, double-click the Text Button to display the **Properties** panel

   ❏ from the Style drop-down menu at the top of the Properties panel, select **[Default Image Button Style]**

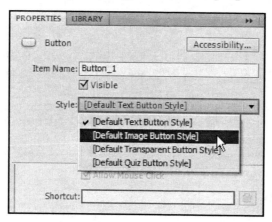

   If you collapse the Properties panel and observe the button on the slide, notice that the button has taken on the Properties of the Default Image Button Style.

---

4. Attach a keyboard shortcut to the button.

   ❑ on Slide 1, double-click the Image Button to display the **Properties** panel

   ❑ from the **Action** group, select the Shortcut field

   ❑ press [**Enter**] on your keyboard

   The word **Enter** appears in the Shortcut field. And just like that, you've made the [Enter] key the shortcut your learners can use to activate the button.

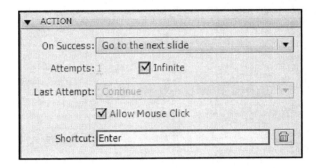

5. Starting on Slide 1, preview the next five slides (**File > Preview**).

6. Run your mouse over the button on Slide 1 and notice the "rollover" effect that is part of the Image button.

7. Press [**Enter**] on your keyboard and, thanks to the keyboard shortcut you attached to the button, you should end up on Slide 2.

8. Close the preview and save your work.

Highlight Boxes

If you want to make sure your users know exactly where they are supposed to look on the screen, you can insert a Drawing Object (as you learned on page 92), or you can insert Highlight Boxes. As with Drawing Objects, you can control the size, color and timing of Highlight Boxes.

Student Activity: Insert and Format a Highlight Box

1. The ButtonHighlightMe project should still be open.

2. Go to **Slide 3**.

3. Edit the style for a Highlight Box.

   ❑ choose **Edit > Object Style Manager**

   ❑ at the far left of the dialog box, click the triangle to expand the **Standard Objects** group

   ❑ select **Highlight Box**

   ❑ from the middle column, select **[Default Blue Highlight Box Style]**

   ❑ from the **Fill & Stroke** area select any Fill, Stroke Color and Width you like (you can change the lightness or darkness of the Fill color by changing the Alpha—the closer you get to 100%, the more opaque the color)

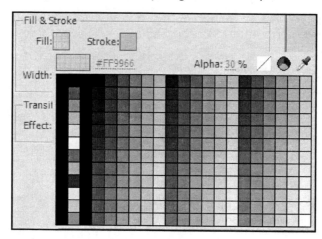

   ❑ change the Transition Effect to **Fade In Only**

   ❑ click the **OK** button

4. Insert a Highlight Box.

    ❏ choose **Insert > Standard Objects > Highlight Box**

    The New Highlight Box dialog box appears using the attributes of the style you just formatted.

5. Resize and reposition the Highlight Box.

    ❏ drag the Highlight Box **up** and to the **left** so that it begins over the **File** menu

    ❏ resize the Highlight Box so that it covers just the **File** menu

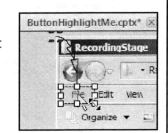

6. Review object timing on the Timeline.

    On the Timeline, notice that the Text Caption and Highlight Box are both set to appear right away and play for 3 seconds. After that, the mouse will appear.

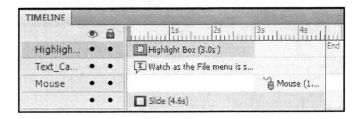

7. Play the slide.

    ❏ choose **File > Preview > Play Slide**

    As expected, the Highlight Box fades in as the slide plays and stays around as long as the text caption. Then the mouse does its thing. However, the timing for the caption is a bit off. You might have noticed that the caption stuck around a bit longer than the Highlight Box. The reason? The Highlight Box has a Fade in only transition. The caption is set to Fade in and Fade out. You'll fix that next.

8. Update and then save changes to an existing style.

    ❏ on Slide 3, double-click the edge of the caption to display the Properties panel

    ❏ from the Transition group, change the **Transition Effect** to **Fade In only**

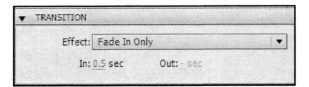

From the Style area at the top of the Properties panel, notice the plus sign to the left of the Default Caption Style. The plus sign indicates changes have been made to the selected caption that do not match the attributes of the style.

☐ click the **Save changes to Existing Style** button

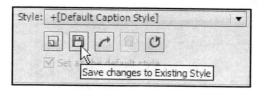

The attributes for all of the captions in the project have been updated and now reflect the Fade In Only Transition Effect.

9. Play the slide.

Now the time and effects for both the Highlight Box and Text Caption match.

10. Save your work.

Confidence Check

1. Go to Slide 5 and insert a Highlight Box and position it over the **New** command.

2. Ensure that the Timeline for the slide matches the picture below.

3. Go to Slide 6 and insert a Highlight Box over the **Folder** command.

4. Select the Caption and choose **Modify > Arrange > Bring to Front**.

5. If necessary, adjust the timing for the slide objects so your Timeline matches the picture below.

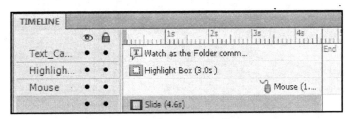

6. Go to Slide 8 and insert a Highlight Box just like you did on **Slide 6**. (Position the Highlight Box over the new folder on the slide.)

7. Bring the Text Caption in front of the Highlight Box.

8. If necessary, adjust the timing for the slide objects so your Timeline matches the picture below.

9. Preview the project to see the Highlight Boxes you've added.

10. When finished, close the preview and save your work.

11. Close the project.

iCONLOGiC

"Skills and Drills" Learning

Module 6: Rollovers and Zoom Areas

In This Module You Will Learn About:

- Rollover Captions, page 110
- Rollover Images, page 114
- Zoom Areas, page 116
- Rollover Slidelets, page 118

And You Will Learn To:

- Insert a Rollover Caption, page 110
- Insert a Rollover Image, page 114
- Insert a Zoom Area, page 116
- Insert and Format a Rollover Slidelet, page 118
- Format the Slidelet, page 120
- Add a Caption and Image to a Slidelet, page 121

Rollover Captions

You learned how to create Text Captions beginning on page 46. While similar to Text Captions, Rollover Captions consist of two things: a caption and a rectangular "hot spot." The Rollover Captions only appear in your published projects if the user moves the mouse over the hot spot. Rollover Captions are especially useful for creating tooltips within an application. For an example of a tooltip in Captivate, point to any tool on the Main toolbar.

Student Activity: Insert a Rollover Caption

1. Using Captivate 5, open **MouseSkills** from the Captivate5EssentialsData folder.

2. Preview the project.

   This project has similar elements such as graphics, buttons and object timing that you have learned to create during previous lessons in this book. During the lessons that follow, you will be adding Rollover Captions to Slide 2 and Rollover Images to Slide 3 of the project.

3. Close the preview.

4. Edit the Default Rollover Area Style.

   ☐ choose **Edit > Object Style Manager**

   ☐ from the top of the Object Style Manager dialog box, expand the Standard Objects (click the triangle to the left of Standard Objects)

   ☐ select **Rollover Area**

   ☐ from the Fill & Stroke area at the right, change the Width to **0**

   ☐ change the Fill color Alpha value to **0%** (the lower the value, the less color you will see... by making it 0, there will not be any Fill color)

   ☐ change the Transition Effect to **No Transition**

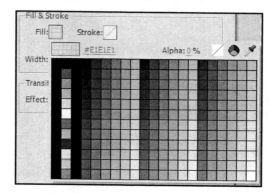

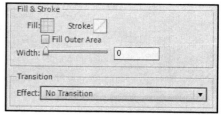

   ☐ click the **OK** button

5. Insert a Rollover Caption on Slide 2.

   ❏ go to **Slide 2**

   ❏ choose **Insert > Standard Objects > Rollover Caption**

   Two things appear on your slide: A Rollover Caption and a Rollover Area. The caption is following the Properties of the already defined Text Captions Style. The Rollover Area is formatted following the Properties you just defined in the Rollover Area style.

   ❏ type **Excellent, you hit number 1!** into the Text Caption

6. Change the caption's Callout Type.

   ❏ deselect all slide objects

   ❏ double-click the edge of the Rollover Caption to display the Properties panel

   ❏ from the General group, change the Callout Type to the first type

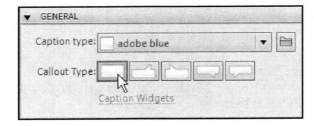

7. Move and resize the Rollover Caption.

   ❏ drag the Rollover Caption just **above** and to the **right** of the image of the number **1**

   ❏ resize the Rollover Caption to suit your taste

8. Move and resize the Rollover Area.

   ❏ drag the **Rollover Area** over the image of the number **1**

   ❏ resize the Rollover Area so that it just covers the image of number **1**

   The position of the Rollover Caption and Rollover Area should look similar to the picture at the right.

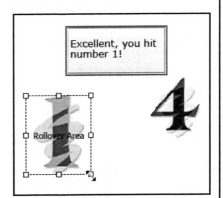

9. Save your work.

Confidence Check

1. Display the Timeline (if necessary).

2. On the Timeline, drag the starting time for the Rollover Area so that the Rollover starts at 3 seconds (the same starting time as the slide images).

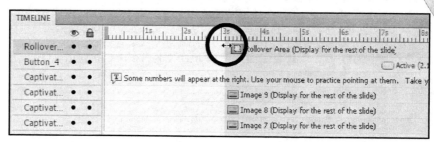

3. Preview the lesson.

4. Once the numbers appear on Slide 2, point to the number 1.

   Your Rollover Caption should appear and disappear as you move your mouse over, and then away from, the number 1.

5. Close the preview.

6. Insert another Rollover Caption on Slide 2 that looks like the picture at the right (Caption Types and Callout Types are up to you).

7. Insert another Rollover Caption that looks like the picture at the right.

8. Insert another Rollover Caption that looks like the picture below.

9. On the Timeline, confirm the timing for the Rollover Captions matches the picture below:

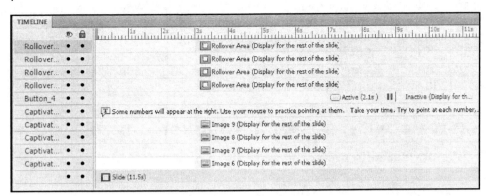

10. Preview the project and confirm that each Rollover Caption appears as expected.

11. When finished, close the preview.

Rollover Images

You learned all about working with images on page 76. Any image you can insert on a slide can instead be a Rollover Image. Similar to Rollover Captions, Rollover Images consist of an image and a rectangular "hot spot." The Rollover Image will only appear in the published project if the user moves the mouse over the hot spot. You might consider using Rollover Images within your projects as a way to offer enhanced views of a dialog box, tool or schematic.

Student Activity: Insert a Rollover Image

1. The **MouseSkills** project should still be open.

2. Insert a Rollover Image on Slide 3.

   ☐ go to **Slide 3**

   ☐ choose **Insert > Standard Objects > Rollover Image**

   ☐ from the **Captivate5EssentialsData\images_animation** folder, open **mouse1.bmp**

   Two things appear on Slide 3: the mouse image (which is the Rollover Image) and a Rollover Area. The Rollover Area is behind the mouse image. The two objects are shown pulled apart in the image below.

   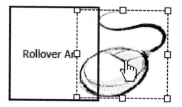

3. Save your work.

Confidence Check

1. Move both the Rollover Area and Rollover Image until your slide looks similar to the picture below.

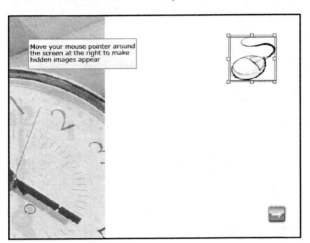

2. Insert a Rollover Image that uses the **mouse2** image.

3. Insert a Rollover Image that uses the **mouse3** image.

4. Move the Rollover Areas until the slide looks similar to this:

5. Preview **In Web Browser** (File > Preview).

6. Test the rollovers on Slides 2 and 3.

7. When finished, close the browser.

8. Save and close the project.

Zoom Areas

You learned how Highlight Boxes can grab the learner's attention on page 104. Zoom Areas offer you an alternative method of grabbing the eye. Zoom Areas consist of two parts: the area you want to highlight and the zoom destination, which shows the enlarged view. During the next activity, you will use a Zoom Area to emphasize a specific tool in an older version of QuarkXPress (a print publishing application similar to Adobe InDesign).

Student Activity: Insert a Zoom Area

1. Using Captivate 5, open **ZoomMe** from the Captivate5EssentialsData folder.

2. Edit the Zoom Source and Zoom Destination Styles.

   ☐ choose **Edit > Object Style Manager**

   ☐ from the top of the Object Style Manager dialog box, expand the Standard Objects (click the triangle to the left of Standard Objects)

   ☐ select **Zoom Source**

   The Zoom Source is what you will use to designate the area of the slide that is going to get larger.

   ☐ from the middle column, select **Default Zoom Source Style** (if necessary)

   ☐ from the **Fill & Stroke** area at the right, change the Width to **0**

   ☐ change the Fill color Alpha to **0%**

   ☐ change the Transition Effect to **No Transition**

   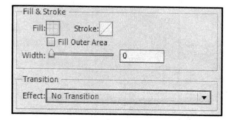

   ☐ select **Zoom Destination** from the list at the left

   The Zoom Destination is where the zoomed area will end up on your slide.

   ☐ from the **Fill & Stroke** area at the right, change the Width to **0**

   ☐ change the Fill color Alpha to **0%**

   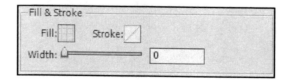

   ☐ click the **OK** button

3. Go to **Slide 13**.

   The caption on the slide says to "Notice that the Content tool is selected..." You will now add a Zoom Area that will display the QuarkXPress Content tool in a larger window.

4. Insert a Zoom Area.

   ❒ still working on Slide 13, choose **Insert > Standard Objects > Zoom Area**

   Two new objects appear in the middle of the slide. One is the **Zoom Destination** and the other is the **Zoom Source**.

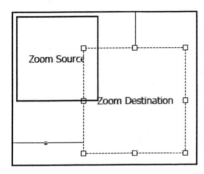

5. Reposition the Zoom Source and Zoom Destination.

   ❒ drag the Zoom Source over the picture of the Content tool on the slide (on the QuarkXPress toolbar shown in the background of Slide 13)

   ❒ resize the Zoom Source so that it is the same size as the Content tool

   ❒ drag the Zoom Destination to the right of the QuarkXPress toolbar

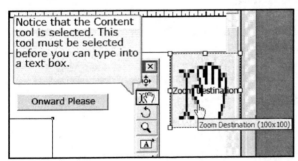

6. Preview the lesson **From this slide** (**File > Preview**).

   Notice that the QuarkXPress Content tool zooms out from the Zoom Source to the Zoom Destination.

7. Close the Preview.

Rollover Slidelets

Rollover Slidelets are basically mini-slides within a slide. Similar to Rollover Captions and Images, Slidelets only appear when the user moves the mouse over a specified area on the slide. Unlike Rollover Captions (which can only contain text) and Rollover Images (which can only contain images), Slidelets can contain images, text, audio, and video. In addition, you can attach navigation controls to a Slidelet.

Student Activity: Insert and Format a Rollover Slidelet

1. The **ZoomMe** project should still be open.

2. Edit the Slidelet and Rollover Slidelet Styles.

   ☐ choose **Edit > Object Style Manager**

   ☐ from the top of the Object Style Manager dialog box, expand the Standard Objects (click the triangle to the left of Standard Objects)

   ☐ select **Slidelet**

   The Slidelet will appear after a learner has clicked or rolled over the Rollover Slidelet. The area can contain images, text, animations and more.

   ☐ from the **Fill & Stroke** area at the right, change the Width to **0**

   ☐ change the Fill color Alpha to **0%**

   ☐ change the Transition Effect to **No Transition**

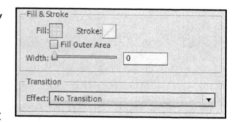

   ☐ select **Rollover Slidelet** from the list at the left

   The Rollover Slidelet is what your learner will click or rollover to display the Slidelet.

   ☐ from the **Fill & Stroke** area at the right, deselect **Show Border**

   ☐ deselect **Show Runtime Border**

   A Runtime Border is optional (it adds a thick border over the Slidelet which I personally find to be a distraction).

   ☐ change the Transition Effect to **No Transition**

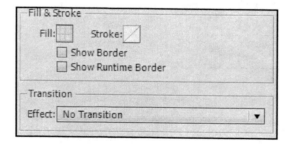

   ☐ click the **OK** button

---

3. Insert a Rollover Slidelet.

    ☐ go to Slide 4

    ☐ choose **Insert > Standard Objects > Rollover Slidelet**

    Two things appear on the slide: the **Rollover Slidelet** and the **Slidelet**.
    While the two objects look similar, the Rollover Slidelet (which is the only one
    of the two objects containing descriptive text) will serve as the hot spot. The
    Slidelet is what will appear should the learner move the mouse over the
    Rollover Slidelet or click it. Although the Rollover Slidelet contains the words
    "Rollover Slidelet," that text will disappear once you make the Rollover Slidelet
    smaller. At that point, you can use your mouse to point at either object to
    display a tooltip that will help you differentiate between the two objects.

4. Move and resize the Rollover Slidelet.

    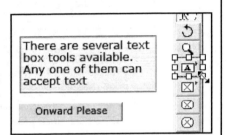

    ☐ drag the Rollover Slidelet over the
    QuarkXPress Rectangle Text Box tool
    on the slide and resize the Rollover Slidelet
    so that it is the same size as the Rectangle
    Text Box tool

5. Set the Rollover Slidelet to "Stick" if clicked.

    ☐ double-click the Rollover Slidelet to display the **Properties panel**
    (as a reminder, the Rollover Slidelet is the smaller of the two objects—the
    one you just positioned and resized)

    ☐ from the Action group, select **Stick Slidelet**

    The Stick Slidelet option means the slidelet will continue to display even when
    the learner moves the mouse away from the Rollover Slidelet. Alternatively,
    you could have selected from a list of On Rollover actions such as Jump to a
    Slide or URL.

    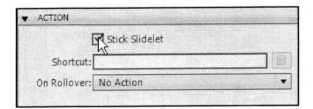

6. Save your work.

Student Activity: Format the Slidelet

1. The **ZoomMe** project should still be open and you should be on **Slide 4**.

2. Change the size and slide position of the Slidelet.

   ☐ double-click the Slidelet to display the **Properties** panel

   ☐ from the **Position & Size** group, deselect **Constrain proportions**

   ☐ change the X value to **44**

   ☐ change the Y value to **120**

   ☐ change the **W** to **230**

   ☐ change the **H** to **176**

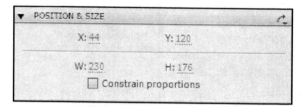

Your Slidelet should be positioned to the left of the Text Caption. Your slide should look like the picture below.

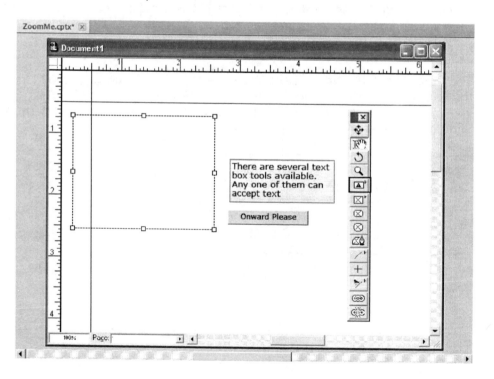

3. Save your work.

Student Activity: Add a Caption and Image to a Slidelet

1. The **ZoomMe** project should still be open and you should be on **Slide 4**.

2. Insert a Text Caption into the Slidelet.

   ❑ select the Slidelet

   Note: If you do not select the Slidelet now, the Text Caption you are about to insert will be inserted on the slide instead of within the Slidelet.

   ❑ choose **Insert > Standard Objects > Text Caption**
   ❑ type **Here are the available Text Box Tools:** into the Text Caption

   The Text Caption has been inserted within the Slidelet. You can move the Text Caption anywhere within the Slidelet, but you cannot drag it outside of the Slidelet.

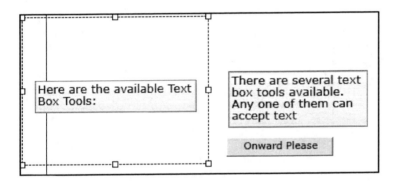

3. Insert an image into the Slidelet.

   ❑ select the Slidelet

   Note: If you do not select the Slidelet now, the image you are about to insert will be inserted onto the slide instead of within the Slidelet.

   ❑ choose **Insert > Image**
   ❑ from the **Captivate5EssentialsData\images_animation** folder, open **AdditionalTextBoxes.jpg**

   As when you inserted the Text Caption, an image has been inserted within the Slidelet. You can move the image anywhere within the Slidelet, but you cannot drag it outside of the Slidelet.

☐ position the image within the Slidelet as shown in the picture below

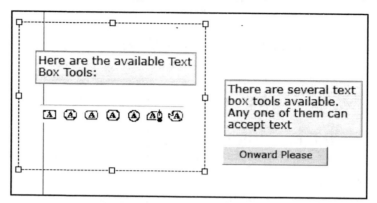

4. Preview five slides.

☐ with Slide 4 selected, choose **File > Preview > Next 5 slides**

5. Use your mouse to point at the Rollover Slidelet you positioned over the QuarkXPress Rectangle Text Box tool.

The Slidelet should appear at the left of the slide with both the Text Caption and image you inserted. If you move your mouse away from the Rollover Slidelet, the Rollover Area will disappear.

6. Close the Preview.

7. Save your work and close the project.

iCONLOGiC
"Skills and Drills" Learning

Module 7: Audio

In This Module You Will Learn About:

- Importing Audio Files, page 124
- Slide Notes, page 127
- Recording Audio, page 128
- Silence, page 135
- Text-to-Speech, page 137

And You Will Learn To:

- Add Audio to a Slide Object, page 124
- Add Background Audio, page 126
- Add a Slide Note, page 127
- Calibrate a Microphone, page 128
- Record a Narration, page 130
- Import Voice Narrations, page 132
- Edit an Audio File, page 133
- Insert Silence, page 135
- Convert Text-to-Speech, page 137

Importing Audio Files

You can add WAV or MP3 sound files to any slide or slide object in a project. If you have a microphone or other recording device attached or built into your computer, you can record your own audio files and use them as voice-overs (also known as narratives). If you have existing audio files, you can import them. When imported, WAV files are converted to MP3 format.

Here is a brief description of the two types of audio files supported by Captivate:

WAV (WAVE): WAV files are one of the original digital audio standards. These kind of files, while of extremely high quality, can be very large. In fact, typical WAV audio files can easily take up to *several megabytes of storage per minute* of playing time. If you have a slow Internet connection, download times for files that large are unacceptable.

MP3 (MPEG Audio Layer III): Developed in Germany by the Fraunhofer Institute, MP3 files are compressed digital audio files. File sizes in this format are typically 90 percent smaller than WAV files.

You can learn more about digital audio formats by visiting **www.webopedia.com/ DidYouKnow/Computer_Science/2005/digital_audio_formats.asp** (a site that details common audio formats).

> **Note:** During the next few activities, you will be working with audio files. To hear the audio or sound effects, your computer must have working speakers or headphones.

Student Activity: Add Audio to a Slide Object

1. Using Captivate 5, open **AudioMe** from the Captivate5EssentialsData folder.

2. Add a sound effect to a Rollover Caption.

   ☐ go to **Slide 2**

   ☐ select the **Excellent, you hit number 1!** caption and choose **Audio > Import to > Object**

   The Import Audio dialog box opens. By default, you should be taken to the Sound folder that comes with Captivate (if not, navigate to the folder where Captivate is installed, open the **Gallery** folder and then open the **Sound** folder).

   ☐ open **Electronic Tink.mp3**

   The Object Audio dialog box appears.

3. Preview the sound.

   ☐ on the Add/Replace tab, click the **Play** button  to hear the audio clip

   ☐ click the **Close** button

   The audio file has been attached to the caption.

Confidence Check

1. Preview the project.

2. When you get to Slide 2, use your mouse to point to Image 1.

   The sound effect should play when the Rollover Caption appears.

3. Close the Preview.

4. Attach sounds to the remaining Rollover Captions on Slide 2.

   Note: You can use any of the sound files available in the **Adobe Captivate 5\Gallery\Sound** folder, or the sound files in the **Captivate5EssentialsData\audio** folder.

   You will also find hundreds of free sound clips online at: **http://www.grsites.com/sounds**.

5. Attach sounds to the Rollover Images on Slide 3.

6. Preview the project. There should be a sound effect attached to each Rollover Caption on Slide 2 and every Rollover Image on Slide 3.

7. When finished, close the preview.

Student Activity: Add Background Audio

1. The **AudioMe** project should still be open.

2. Import an audio file that plays for the entire project.

   ☐ choose **Audio > Import to > Background**

   ☐ from the **Captivate5EssentialsData\audio** folder, open **2Step1.mp3**

   The Background Audio dialog box opens.

   ☐ from the Options area of the Add/Replace tab, ensure that **Loop Audio** is selected

   The audio file you imported is large enough to play for just over one minute. By selecting Loop Audio, the music will play over and over again. Using this technique, you can use smaller audio files for background music and keep the size of your published lesson as small as possible.

   ☐ ensure that **Stop audio at end of project** is selected

   This option ensures that the background music stops when the project is closed by a learner.

   ☐ ensure that **Adjust background audio volume on slides with audio** is selected

   This option ensures that the sound effects you added to Slides 2 and 3 are still audible even though the background music will be playing.

   ☐ ensure that the slider at the right is set to **50%**

   When adjusting the background audio on slides with audio, the slider controls how much the background audio volume will lower. The 50% setting is the default.

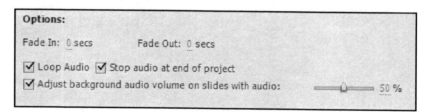

   ☐ click the **Close** button

3. Preview the project.

   You should be able to hear the background music and, when you get to the slides with the sound effects attached to objects, you should still be able to hear the sound effects.

4. Close the preview.

5. Save your work and close the project.

Slide Notes

Slide Notes can serve multiple functions. For instance, if you are working with a team of Captivate developers and sharing the Captivate projects, you can add Slide Notes that will serve as production comments. If you elect to publish your project as a Word document, the Notes can be included and appear within the Word document. And, because Slide Notes can be displayed when you record voice-overs in Captivate, you can use the Slide Notes as a digital narration script. During the next activity, you will use the Slide Notes feature to add a narration script that you'll use when recording your voice in just a few moments.

Student Activity: Add a Slide Note

1. Open **NarrateMe** from the Captivate5EssentialsData folder.

2. Open the Slide Notes panel.

   ❑ go to **Slide 2**

   ❑ choose **Window > Slide Notes**

   At the bottom of the slide, notice there is a panel where you can add Closed Captions, convert Text-to speech and add Slide Notes.

   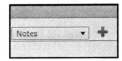

3. Add a Slide Note.

   ❑ click the plus sign 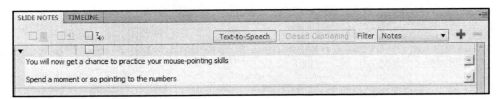 to add a Slide Note

   ❑ type **You will now get a chance to practice your mouse-pointing skills**

   ❑ press [**enter**] twice

   ❑ type **Spend a moment or so pointing to the numbers**

4. Save your work.

Recording Audio

Captivate allows you to record your own audio and sound effects and insert them three ways: you can attach audio to an entire lesson (running in the background), to an individual slide, or to any object on the slide.

If you plan to record your own audio, you will first need a microphone connected to your computer. After the microphone, consider the following:

Setup: If you plan to use high-end audio hardware such as a mixer or preamplifier, plug your microphone into the hardware and then plug the hardware into your computer's "line in" port. Set the volume on your mixer or preamplifier to just under zero (this will minimize distortion).

Microphone placement: The microphone should be positioned 4 to 6 inches from your mouth to reduce the chance that nearby sounds will be recorded. Ideally, you should position the microphone above your nose and pointed down at your mouth. Also, if you position the microphone just to the side of your mouth you can soften the sound of the letters S and P.

Microphone technique: It's a good idea to keep a glass of water close and, just before recording, take a drink. To eliminate the annoying breathing and lip smack sounds, turn away from the microphone, take a deep breath, exhale, take another deep breath, open your mouth, turn back toward the microphone, and start speaking. Speak slowly. When recording for the first time, many people race through the content. Take your time.

Student Activity: Calibrate a Microphone

1. The **NarrateMe** project should still be open.

2. Select a Bitrate.

   ❑ still working on **Slide 2**, choose **Audio > Record to > Slide**

   The Slide Audio dialog box appears.

   ❑ on the Add/Replace tab, click the **Settings** button

   The Audio Settings dialog box appears.

   ❑ ensure that your microphone is selected from the **Audio Input Devices, Select** drop-down menu

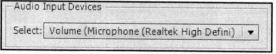

   ❑ ensure that **Constant Bitrate** is selected from the Bitrate drop-down menu

   Constant Bitrates (CBRs) produce consistent and predictably smaller file sizes. By contrast, Variable Bitrates (VBRs) tend to produce audio with a higher, more consistent quality level than CBRs but the VBR file sizes will be larger than CBRs.

❏ if necessary, change the Encoding Bitrate to **FM Bitrate (64kbps)**

Using a higher Encoding Bitrate setting will result in larger published lessons. If you decide to use a higher quality bitrate than FM Bitrate, you should spend time experimenting with these options to see which selection sounds best to you. As a general rule, the FM Bitrate is more than adequate for audio that will be played through typical computer speakers or headsets.

3. Calibrate a microphone.

❏ click the **Calibrate Input** button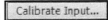

The **Calibrate audio input** dialog box appears. This is where you can set your microphone to its optimum recording level and sensitivity.

❏ click the **Auto calibrate** button

❏ speaking slowly and clearly, say:

I am setting my microphone recording level for use with Adobe Captivate

❏ when the words **Input Level OK** appear in green, you can stop speaking

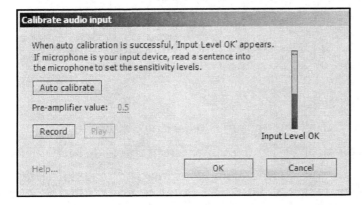

❏ click each of the two **OK** buttons (one to close the Calibrate audio input dialog box and another to close the Audio settings dialog box).

You should be back at the Slide Audio dialog box, ready to record your audio.

Student Activity: Record a Narration

1. The **NarrateMe** project should still be open and you should have calibrated your microphone following the steps on page 128.

2. Practice the recording.

   ❐ click the **Captions & Slide Notes** button at the bottom of the dialog box

   The Notes you created on page 127 appear in a dialog box. You can move the dialog box anywhere on your monitor that is comfortable to you.

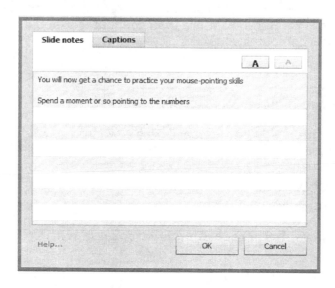

   ❐ with the Slide notes tab selected, take a deep breath and, using a not-too-fast cadence, read the Slide Note out loud for practice:

   You will now get a chance to practice your mouse-pointing skills. Spend a moment or so pointing to the numbers

3. Record a narration.

   ❐ get in front of a microphone (or other recording device)

   ❐ click the **Record** button ⊙ in the upper left of the Slide Audio dialog box

   ❐ after the countdown goes away, take your time and read the Slide Note again: **You will now get a chance to practice your mouse-pointing skills. Spend a moment or so pointing to the numbers**

   ❐ when finished, click the **Stop** button ▣ (located just to the right of the Record button)

   ❐ click the **OK** button to close the Slide notes dialog box

4. Preview the audio.

   ❐ click the **Play Audio** button ▶ located just to the right of the Stop button

Confidence Check

1. If you are happy with the narration, click the **Save** button and then click the **Close** button.

   If not, on the Add/Replace tab, click the **Record** button again and rerecord the audio. When finished, click the **Save** button and then click the **Close** button.

2. On the Filmstrip, notice that the thumbnail for Slide 2 contains a tiny speaker icon, an indication that audio has been added to the slide.

3. Preview the project.

   Notice that when you get to Slide 2, the background audio lowers automatically and you can hear your narration.

4. Close the preview

5. Save your work.

6. Close the project.

Student Activity: Import Voice Narrations

1. Open **EditMyAudio** from the Captivate5EssentialsData folder.

   This file is similar to the file you just closed, except it does not contain any slide audio or notes.

2. Import a prerecorded voice narration to Slide 2.

   ☐ go to Slide 2

   ☐ choose **Audio > Import to > Slide**

   ☐ from the **audio** folder, open **oops_somenumber.wav**

   Because the audio file you just imported is longer than the current slide timing, the **Audio Import Options** dialog box appears. You have three options: make the slide timing match the length of the imported audio, force the audio to play over multiple slides, or split the audio equally among all of the slides in the project.

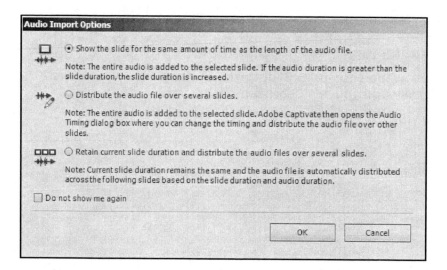

   ☐ ensure **Show the slide for the same amount of time as the length of the audio file** is selected

   ☐ click the **OK** button

3. Preview the project.

   When you get to Slide 2, you should hear a bit of a problem. The person being recorded did not know the recording had begun and the audio includes a bit of a gaffe. Normally, you'd have to open the audio file in an audio editing program, make the changes and re-import the audio back into Captivate. Instead, you can use the audio editing features within Captivate to delete the unwanted portions of the audio now.

4. Save your work.

Student Activity: Edit an Audio File

1. The **EditMyAudio** project should still be open.

2. Edit an audio clip.

   ❏ display the Timeline for Slide 2 (Window > Timeline)

   ❏ at the bottom of the Timeline, **double-click** the waveform (the waveform is the squiggly line at the bottom of the Timeline) to display the Edit Audio dialog box

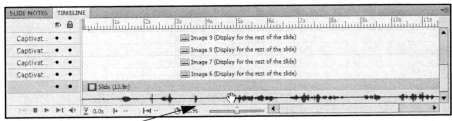

The Waveform

   ❏ if necessary, drag the Timeline's **Zoom** slider **left** so that you can see more of the waveform

3. Identify and select the problem areas of the waveform.

   ❏ click **anywhere on the waveform**

   ❏ click in the beginning of the waveform

   ❏ drag **right** to select the first third (approximately 4 seconds) of the waveform

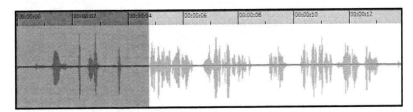

   ❏ click the **Play/Pause** button ▶

   Your goal is to select just the part of the waveform that contains the audio gaffe (you'll be deleting the selection). If you have selected too much or too little of the audio, go ahead and drag left or right as necessary until you've only selected the part of the audio that needs to be deleted. Click the Play/ Pause button to confirm your selection when finished.

4. Delete the audio gaffe.

   ❏ click the **Delete** tool 🗑

   The unwanted portion of the audio should be gone.

   ❏ click the **Play/Pause** button ▶ to hear the edited audio

   ❏ click the **Save** button and then click the **Close** button

Confidence Check

1. Edit the audio again. This time, delete the dead air at the end of the waveform—the last **half second or so** (it's a good idea to play the selection prior to deleting it).

2. When finished, click the **Save** button and then click the **Close** button.

3. Go to Slide 3 and import the **move_mouse_pointer.wav** audio to the slide.

4. Edit the imported audio, removing the dead air at the very beginning of the waveform and at the end.

5. Preview the project to hear the audio you've added so far.

6. When finished previewing, close the preview and save your work.

7. *Here's something cool:* Choose **Audio > Audio Management**.

   The Advanced Audio Management dialog box appears. You can use this dialog box to review the audio being used on every object on every slide, play audio and delete the audio.

8. Select **Show object level audio** (at the bottom left of the dialog box) to see a listing of every audio file used in the project.

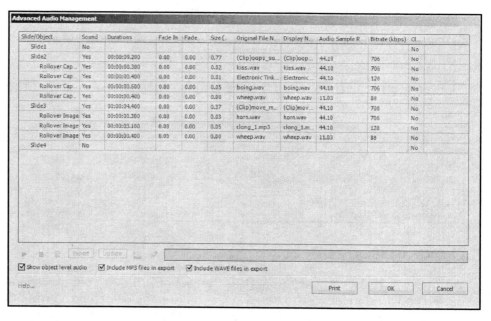

Slide/Object	Sound	Durations	Fade In	Fade	Size (.	Original File N...	Display N...	Audio Sample R...	Bitrate (kbps)	Cl...
Slide1	No									No
Slide2	Yes	00:00:09.200	0.00	0.00	0.77	(Clip)oops_so...	(Clip)oop...	44.10	706	No
Rollover Cap...	Yes	00:00:00.300	0.00	0.00	0.02	kiss.wav	kiss.wav	44.10	706	No
Rollover Cap...	Yes	00:00:00.400	0.00	0.00	0.01	Electronic Tink...	Electronic...	44.10	128	No
Rollover Cap...	Yes	00:00:00.600	0.00	0.00	0.05	boing.wav	boing.wav	44.10	706	No
Rollover Cap...	Yes	00:00:00.400	0.00	0.00	0.00	wheep.wav	wheep.wav	11.03	88	No
Slide3	Yes	00:00:04.400	0.00	0.00	0.37	(Clip)move_m...	(Clip)mov...	44.10	706	No
Rollover Image	Yes	00:00:00.300	0.00	0.00	0.03	horn.wav	horn.wav	44.10	706	No
Rollover Image	Yes	00:00:03.180	0.00	0.00	0.05	clong_1.mp3	clong_1.m...	44.10	128	No
Rollover Image	Yes	00:00:00.400	0.00	0.00	0.00	wheep.wav	wheep.wav	11.03	88	No
Slide4	No									No

☑ Show object level audio ☑ Include MP3 files in export ☑ Include WAVE files in export

Help...   Print   OK   Cancel

9. Select any audio file you like and click the **Export** button at the bottom of the dialog box.

   You could now specify a folder and export any audio file from your project. This is an especially useful feature if you have recorded audio files directly in Captivate, edited them and then need to use them in other programs.

10. Cancel the export and Cancel the Advanced Audio Management dialog box.

11. Save and close the project.

Silence

One of the things you will come across most often in audio files is those annoying lip smacks. If you are the one recording the audio, you can take steps to avoid inevitable lip smacking by wetting your lips just prior to recording the audio. Of course, if you have inherited lip-smack audio, never fear. You can use Captivate's Insert Silence feature to eliminate parts of an audio waveform without changing the duration of the audio.

Student Activity: Insert Silence

1. Open **SilenceMe** from the Captivate5EssentialsData folder.

2. Go to **Slide 2** and, if necessary, show the Timeline.

3. On the Timeline, double-click the waveform (the waveform is the bottom object on the Timeline)

4. Click at the beginning of the audio clip and then click the **Play/Pause** tool.

   Listen carefully, and you will notice that there are actually three lip smacks in the audio. If you zoom closer to the waveform, you can actually see them (the lip smacks are the small blips you see in the valleys between the major waves as indicated by the mouse pointer in the image below).

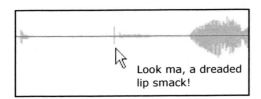

Look ma, a dreaded lip smack!

5. Insert Silence.

   ❏ using your mouse, select the area just before and after the lip smack on the waveform

   ❏ click the **Insert Silence** button

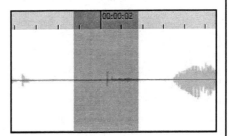

The lip smack... gone!

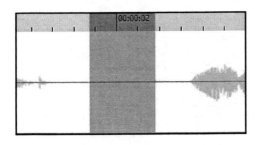

Confidence Check

1. Replace the remaining two lip smacks with silence.

2. Click the **Save** button and then click the **Close** button.

3. Preview the project.

4. When finished, save your work.

Text-to-Speech

Artificial voices have been around for years. In fact, there are many applications that will allow you to select text and then have Text-to-Speech software convert the selected text into an audio file.

The problem with artificial voices was, well, the voices sounded artificial. Today's Text-to-Speech technology has made huge strides. While not perfect, the artificial voices sound more human than ever before.

Why consider artificial voices over recorded audio? Great question. If you record the audio yourself, you should budget several hours to clean up the audio (removing lip smacks and static in the background). In spite of your best efforts, the audio files you create might still be considered less than adequate. And consider the fact that your voice changes over the day. If you need to replace a small segment in a larger clip, you will find it nearly impossible to match the audio levels without sophisticated and expensive audio equipment. By using artificial voices, you can ensure that the audio levels and quality are always consistent. And your artificial talent never gets sick, never takes a vacation, never ages and will never, ever, give you any attitude.

> **Note:** Before you can take full advantage of Captivate's voices, you will need to install them. The voice installers (there are two) are typically found in the **Adobe Captivate 5 Content\Add-ons** folder that is part of the Captivate 5 installation files. There is an installer for **Neospeech** (which adds two voices, Paul and Kate); and an installer for **Loquendo** (which provides three new voices, Stefan, Juliette and Simon). You can learn more by visiting the Adobe Captivate Blog (**http:// blogs.adobe.com/captivate/2010/05/announcing_new_text-to-speech.html**).

Student Activity: Convert Text-to-Speech

1. The SilenceMe.cp project should still be open.

2. Convert a slide note to speech.

   ☐ go to **Slide 2** and open the Slide Notes panel (Window > Slide Notes)

   ☐ click the **Text-to-Speech** Button

   ☐ select a Speech Agent from the drop-down menu

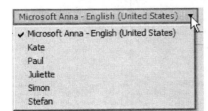

   ☐ click the **Add Text-to-Speech** button ➕

   ☐ type: **You will now get a chance to practice your mouse-pointing skills.**

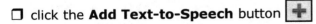
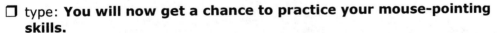
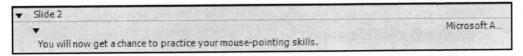

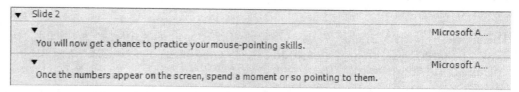

❏ click the **Add Text to Speech** button

❏ type: **Once the numbers appear on the screen, spend a moment or so pointing to them.**

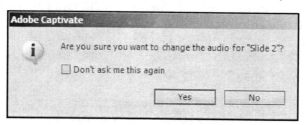

▼ Slide 2	
▼	Microsoft A...
You will now get a chance to practice your mouse-pointing skills.	
▼	Microsoft A...
Once the numbers appear on the screen, spend a moment or so pointing to them.	

❏ click the **Generate Audio** button [Generate Audio]

❏ click **Yes** when asked if you want to replace the audio on the slide

Adobe Captivate

ⓘ Are you sure you want to change the audio for "Slide 2"?

☐ Don't ask me this again

[Yes]   [No]

❏ click the **Close** button

3. Save your work.

4. Preview the project. When you get to Slide 2, you will hear your new Text-to-Speech audio narration. *How cool is that?*

Note: The Text-to-Speech audio can be edited like any of the other audio clips you learned to edit during this module. In addition, you can change the voice from one agent to the next, and then back again simply by choosing Audio > Speech Management. Change the Speech Agent and click Generate Audio.

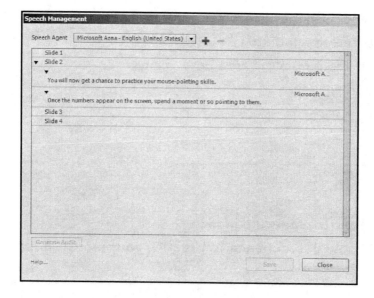

5. Save and close the project.

iCONLOGiC

"Skills and Drills" Learning

Module 8: Flash Video, Animation and Effects

In This Module You Will Learn About:

- Flash Video, page 140
- Animation, page 144
- Text Animation, page 146
- Object Effects, page 148

And You Will Learn To:

- Insert Flash Video, page 140
- Set Flash Video Properties, page 141
- Add Animation to a Slide, page 144
- Insert Text Animation, page 146
- Apply a Fly-In Effect to a Text Caption, page 148
- Apply a ZigZag Motion Path, page 149

Flash Video

You can add Flash Video files (FLV or F4V) to your Captivate projects.
When importing the video, you can elect to import directly from your computer or import a file that is already stored on a Web server (Flash Video Streaming Service or Flash Media Server).

Student Activity: Insert Flash Video

1. Open **AnimateMe** from the Captivate5EssentialsData folder.

2. Go to Slide 1.

   You will be adding a Flash Video that fits in the white space at the left of the logo on the slide.

3. Insert a Flash Video.

   ❑ choose **Insert > FLV or F4V File**

   The Import Video dialog box appears.

   ❑ ensure that **On your Computer** is selected from the Where is your video file? area

   ❑ click the **Browse** button at the right

   ❑ navigate to **Captivate5EssentialsData\images_animation**

   ❑ open **welcomeToLesson.flv**

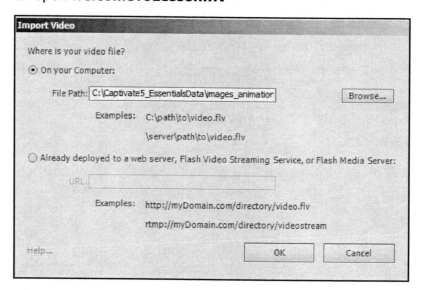

   ❑ click the **OK** button

   The video is imported, but it is too big for the slide.

4. Save your work.

Student Activity: Set Flash Video Properties

1. The AnimateMe.cptx project should still be open.

2. Change the size of the video.

   ❑ double-click the video on Slide 1 to show the Properties panel

   ❑ from the **Position & Size** group of the Properties panel, ensure that **Constrain proportions** is selected

   ❑ change the **W** to **200** and then click in the H field

   Thanks to Constrain proportions, the Height of the video automatically changes to 150.

   ❑ still working on the **Position & Size** group, change the **X** to **121** and the **Y** to **129**

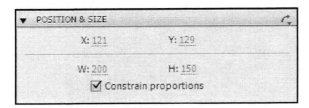

   Your slide should look like the picture below.

3. Preview the next 5 slides.

   A box where the video should play appears, but the video does not play. In addition, before you know it, the next slide appears. You'll fix a few problems next.

4. Close the Preview.

5. Change the display timing and transition effect for the video.

❑ double-click the video on Slide 1 to show the Properties panel and then open the **Timing** group

❑ from the **Display For** drop-down menu, select **rest of slide**

❑ ensure that **Pause slide till end of video** is selected

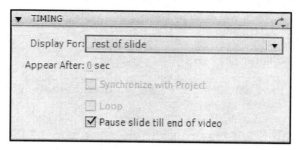

The **Pause slide till end of video** option will ensure that the first slide sticks around long enough for the video to play.

❑ open the Transition group

❑ from the **Effect** drop-down menu, select **No Transition**

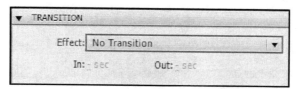

Using Transitions is always optional. However, I tend to shy away from them unless they are adding value to the lesson.

6. Preview the next 5 slides.

This time the box containing the video appears, but the slide does not move on to Slide 2 on its own.

7. On the video's Playbar, click the **Play** button to play the video.

A guide walks onto the screen, introduces the lesson and then exits, stage right.

8. Close the Preview.

9. Change the video's Playbar and force the video to play automatically.

   ❑ double-click the video on Slide 1 to show the Properties panel and then open the General group at the top of the panel

   ❑ select **Auto Play**

   ❑ from the Skin drop-down menu, select **clearSkin1**

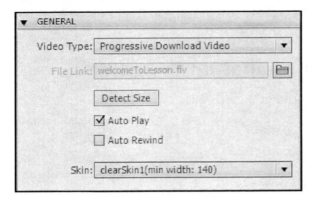

   ❑ on the Position & Size group, change the **X** to **132** and the **Y** to **130**

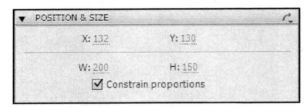

10. Preview the next 5 slides.

   Notice that the shell (the skin) surrounding the video has been changed and that the video plays automatically once the slide appears.

11. Close the Preview.

12. Save your work.

Animation

During the first activity in this module, you learned to import FLV videos. But you can also import animations in either the Flash (SWF) or Animated GIF (GIF) format.
If you have the time, software and ability you can create your own animations and import them into Captivate. You can also search the Web for animations. However, if you go the Web route, check for copyright restrictions on the animations you find. Thankfully, Captivate ships with several animations. You'll find those free animations in the **SWF Animation** folder.

Student Activity: Add Animation to a Slide

1. The AnimateMe project should still be open.

2. Insert an animation.

    ❑ go to **Slide 2**

    ❑ choose **Insert > Animation**

    You should already be looking within the SWF Animation folder. If not, navigate there now.

    ❑ open the **Arrows** folder

    ❑ open the **Blue Fade** folder

    ❑ open **downright.swf**

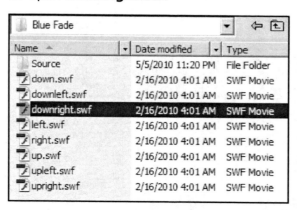

    The animation shows up on your slide as a box containing the word "Animation." Next, you will change the animation's slide position and timing.

3. Save your work.

Confidence Check

1. With the AnimateMe project still open, drag the Animation closer to the button at the right of the slide.

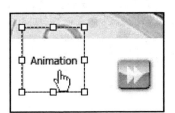

2. Double-click the animation on **Slide 2** to show the Properties panel.

3. From the **Position & Size** group, change the **X** to **504** and the **Y** to **83**

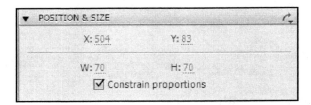

The animation should now be located just above and to the left of the button on the slide.

4. Preview the Next 5 Slides and notice that the timing of the animation on Slide 2 needs work. It would be better if the animation appeared around the same time as the button (currently the animation appears right away but the button does not appear until after 4 seconds).

5. Show the animation's Properties again.

6. From the Timing group, change the Display For to **rest of slide**.

7. Change the Appear After to **5** sec.

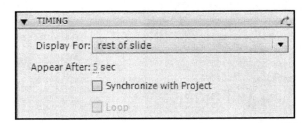

8. From the Transition group, change the Transition Effect to **No Transition**.

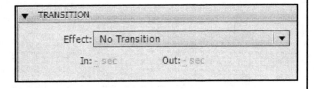

9. Preview the Next 5 Slides and notice that the timing of the animation is now better.

10. Spend a moment or two inserting some other animations that come with Captivate.

11. Save your work (keep the project open for the next activity).

Text Animation

Text Animations are Flash objects that you can insert on your slides that can bring static text to life (you won't need to know Flash to use Text Animations). There are more than 90 Text Animations from which to choose. While cool, I would recommend you use Text Animation's sparingly since they can quickly become a distraction.

Student Activity: Insert Text Animation

1. The AnimateMe project should still be open.

2. On **Slide 2**, delete the **Lesson 1: Creating New Folders** image currently on the slide. (You're about to insert a text animation in its place.)

3. Insert Text Animation.

   ❏ still working on Slide 2, choose **Insert > Text Animation**

   The Text Animation Properties dialog box appears.

   ❏ replace the words Sample Text with **Creating New Folders**

   ❏ change the Font to Verdana

   ❏ change the Size to **36**

   ❏ click the **OK** button

   The animation appears on the slide.

   ❏ reposition the animation until its slide position is similar to the image below

4. Save your work.

5. Change animation effects.

❏ on Slide 2, click once on the text animation you just moved

❏ choose **Window > Properties** to display the Properties panel (if necessary)

❏ from the General group, Effect drop-down menu, select **DePlume**

You will see a sample of the effect at the top of the Properties panel.

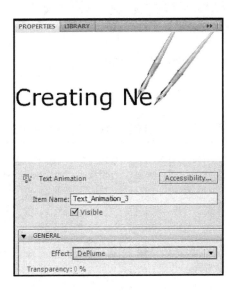

❏ select **Red_Hot_Skew** from the Effect drop-down menu

Once again you will see a sample of the effect in the area at the top of the panel.

❏ select **Trailing_Light** from the Effect drop-down menu

Confidence Check

1. From the Timing group, change the **Display For** to **rest of slide** and change the **Appear After** to **3 sec**.

2. From the Transition group, change the Transition to **No Transition**.

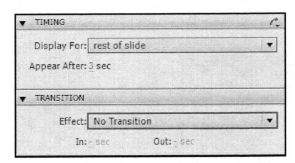

3. Preview the project to see the text animation in action. When finished, close the preview, save your work and close the project.

Object Effects

You have now learned how to add videos (FLVs, page 140), animation (page 144) and text animation (page 146). But you can also apply myriad effects to selected slide objects without ever leaving Captivate. In fact, you can right-click any slide object and choose Apply Effect. From there, you can use the Effects panel to add, remove and control the timing of several effects that come with Captivate.

Student Activity: Apply a Fly-In Effect to a Text Caption

1. Open **EffectMe** from the Captivate5EssentialsData folder.

2. Go to Slide 3.

   There are four text captions on the slide. You are about to apply two effects to the first one. The slide position of the caption is important. The first effect you will apply will have a caption fly in from the right side of the screen. As the caption performs the Effect, it will fly in from the far right of the slide as instructed and stop at the designated slide position.

3. Apply a Fly-In Effect to a Text Caption.

   ☐ on Slide 3, right-click the text caption containing the words "During this demonstration..." and choose **Apply Effect**

   The Effects panel appears at the bottom of your window (it's grouped with the Timeline by default).

   ☐ in the lower left of the Effects panel, click the **Add Effect** button

   ☐ select **Entrance > Fly In > Fly In From Right**

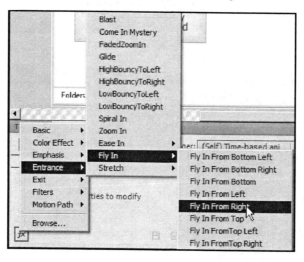

4. Preview the Next 5 Slides.

   As expected, the text caption appears from the right side of the screen and stops in its original slide position.

5. Close the Preview and save your work.

Student Activity: Apply a ZigZag Motion Path

1. The **EffectMe** project should still be open.

2. Apply a ZigZag Effect to a Text Caption.

   ❏ still working on Slide 3, and with the text caption containing the words "During this demonstration..." selected, click the **Add Effect** button

   ❏ choose **Motion Path > ZigZag**

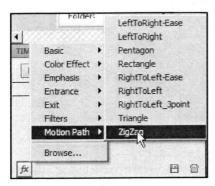

   Notice on the Effects panel that both effects appear. However, unless you do something about it, the effects will play at the same time.

3. Change the timing for an Effect.

   ❏ on the Effects panel, drag the ZigZag effect right until its left edge lines up at the 7s mark (you'll find that working with the Effects panel is similar to working with the Timeline, which you learned about on page 59)

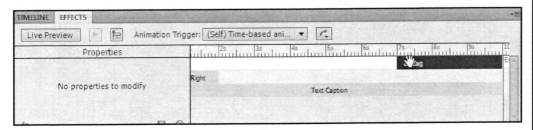

4. Save your work.

5. Preview the Next 5 Slides.

   Nice effect, sort of! The caption flies in from the right and stops. Then after a few seconds, it starts zigging and zagging... and then stops. You'll need to control the zig zags a little bit more so the caption goes right and leaves the slide completely.

Confidence Check

1. Still working on Slide 3 of the EffectMe project, select the Text Caption containing both of the Effects (the one starting with the words "During this...")

2. Notice the number 1 that appears in the lower right of the selected Text Caption? Excellent! Click the number **1** to reveal the current ZigZag motion path.

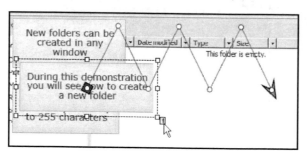

3. Drag the green arrow at the right of the motion path **right** and just off the slide.

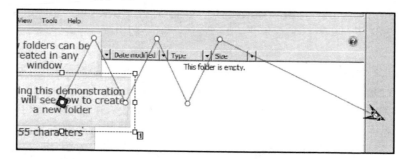

4. Drag the white dots at the top and bottom of the path to change the height of each zig and zag.

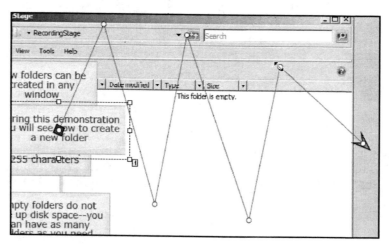

5. Preview the Next 5 Slides to see your changes.

   Happy with your work? Save and close. Not happy? Spend a few minutes tweaking the motion path and preview. Once satisfied, save and close the project.

iCONLOGiC

"Skills and Drills" Learning

Module 9: Click and Text Entry Boxes

In This Module You Will Learn About:

- Demonstrations versus Simulations, page 152
- Find and Replace, page 153
- Click Boxes, page 155
- Text Entry Boxes, page 159

And You Will Learn To:

- Hide the Mouse, page 152
- Replace Phrases, page 153
- Insert a Click Box, page 155
- Insert a Text Entry Box, page 159

Demonstrations versus Simulations

The two most common types of eLearning that developers create with Captivate are software demonstrations and simulations. So far you have focused on creating and cleaning up demonstrations—projects that are intended to demonstrate a concept. You added some interactivity to a project when you learned about Text and Image Buttons (page 99). Nevertheless, the projects you have learned to create so far have not encouraged user interaction. Anyone watching a demonstration would be expected to merely sit back and watch slide objects appear on the screen and watch the mouse move around the slide. Although there is nothing wrong with demonstrations, simulations can improve the learning experience by letting users actively participate in the lesson.

Most people who teach themselves Captivate create demonstrations. Why? The most common answers I will hear to that question are: 1) I didn't know how to create a simulation; and 2) I thought creating a simulation would be too hard. After this module you will know how to create simulations from scratch. As for difficulty, simulations can take a bit longer to produce than demonstrations, but they are not difficult to create.

I've spent years teaching Captivate. After I teach my students how to create killer simulations in Captivate, I often hear that the new skills are greeted with mixed emotions. Students are happy that they'll now be able to create more effective lessons, but they're bummed out that the work they put into creating the demonstrations was wasted time. Not so! If you've created good demonstrations, there is no need to throw them away. During the lessons that follow, I will teach you how to add Click Boxes and Text Entry Fields to your projects that will quickly convert your existing demonstrations into simulations.

Student Activity: Hide the Mouse

1. Open **ConvertMeToSimulation** from the Captivate5EssentialsData folder.

   On the Filmstrip, notice that there is a **mouse icon** in the lower right of Slides 3 through 9. The mouse icon is a visual indicator that the mouse pointer is appearing on the slide and is a quick way to determine that this is a demonstration project. It has been saved with a new name so that it can be converted into a simulation. The first step to converting a demonstration into a simulation would be to hide the mouse on all of the slides. You will do that next.

2. Hide the mouse for the entire project.

   ❏ select **Slide 3**

   ❏ press [**shift**] on your keyboard and then click one time on **Slide 9**

   ❏ release [**shift**]

   Slides 3 through 9 should now be selected.

   ❏ choose **Modify > Mouse > Show Mouse** (to turn the Show Mouse command off)

   The mouse pointer has been hidden on each of the selected slides.

Find and Replace

While you can use Captivate's Find and Replace dialog box to find any object in your project (including images, animation and Flash video), you will find it is most useful as a tool for finding and replacing words or phrases in your Text Captions. Without this ability, the process of making global text changes in a project would be very tedious.

During the following activity, you will use Captivate's Find and Replace feature to replace passive phrases with active phrases—an important component of simulations.

Student Activity: Replace Phrases

1. The ConvertMeToSimulation project should still be open.

2. Go to Slide 3.

   Notice that the text in the Text Caption (**Watch as the File menu is selected**) is written in the *passive voice*. While writing in the passive voice is acceptable for demonstrations, the most effective way to write interactive instructions is in the *active voice*.

3. Replace a phrase in Text Captions.

   ❏ choose **Edit > Find and Replace**

   The Find and Replace panel opens.

   ❏ if necessary, select **Text Caption** from the Search In drop-down menu and ensure that **All Styles** is selected from the Style drop-down menu

   ❏ type **Watch as** into the Find field

   ❏ type **Select** into the Replace field

   Ensure that you typed both entries exactly as written above and have matched the case.

   ❏ select **Match Case** from the two options at the left of the dialog box

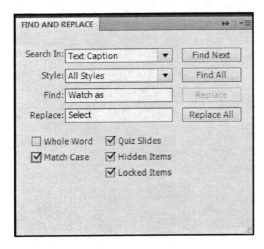

   ❏ click the **Find Next** button

The first occurrence of the phrase you typed into the Find field is found and highlighted.

❐ click the **Replace All** button

You will be alerted that 4 instances of the phrase have been found and replaced.

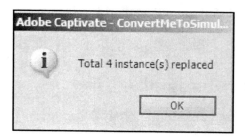

❐ click the **OK** button

4. Save your work.

Confidence Check

1. Use the Find and Replace feature to delete the phrase **is selected** from all of the Text Captions.

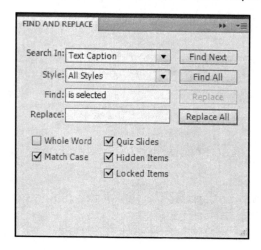

You should be alerted of 4 more changes to your project.

2. Save your work.

Click Boxes

Instead of telling and then showing a learner how to perform an action, you can insert Click Boxes that allow the learner to perform actions such as clicking a menu or menu command.

Student Activity: Insert a Click Box

1. The ConvertMeToSimulation project should still be open.

2. Preview the project.

   There is an interactive button on the first slide. Clicking the button will take you to Slide 2. From this point forward, there is no interactivity in the project.

3. Close the preview.

4. Insert a Click Box on Slide 3.

   ❏ go to Slide 3

   ❏ choose **Insert > Standard Objects > Click Box**

   A new Click Box appears in the middle of your screen. The mouse badge on the lower right of the Click Box, while small, contains valuable information. If you look closely, you will see a green icon on the left side of the mouse badge indicating that the Click Box will be activated with a left click. You can use the Click Box Properties to set the box to the right-clickable, in which case the right side of the mouse badge would be green.

5. Change the On Success action for the Click Box.

   ❏ double-click the Click Box to display the Properties panel

   ❏ from the top of the **Action** group, **On Success** drop-down menu, choose **Go to the next slide**

   ❏ from the **Attempts** area, ensure that **Infinite** is selected

6. Add a Failure Caption to the Click Box.

   ❏ ensure that the Properties panel for the Click Box is still open

   ❏ from the Options group, Captions area, select **Failure**

   ❏ ensure that the remaining options match the picture at the right

   The **Failure Caption** option will insert a Failure Caption on the slide for you. This is the caption that will appear if the learner does not click on the Click Box.

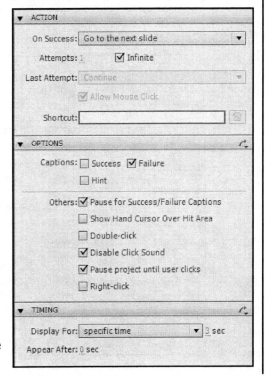

The **Pause for Success/Failure Caption** ensures that the learner is given a chance to read the Failure Caption before getting frustrated and clicking again in the wrong place. The Disable Click Sound will ensure that the learner won't hear a double-click sound when they click the Click Box (their click and one created by the Click Box). And by selecting **Pause project until user clicks**, you ensure that the project will not continue unless the user clicks the Click Box.

7. Reposition the Click Box.

   ☐ **drag** the Click Box **up** and to the **left** so that the upper left of the Click Box is over the word "File" in the File menu on the slide background

   ☐ resize the Click Box so that it covers the word "File" in the File menu

8. Save your work.

9. Position the Failure Caption on the slide.

   ☐ drag the Failure Caption to the right of the Click Box you just resized

10. Edit the Failure Caption's text, and select a Callout Type.

    ☐ double-click the Failure Caption to enter Text Editing mode

    ☐ replace the text with the phrase **Click here**

    ☐ on the Properties panel, General group, select the third Callout Type

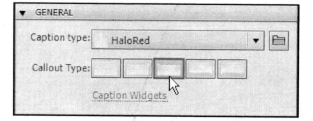

11. Position the Failure Caption so that its slide position is similar to the picture below.

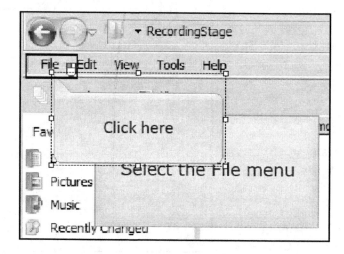

Confidence Check

1. Save your work and then Preview the project from Slide 3.

2. Test the Failure Caption by clicking anywhere except the File menu.

3. Close the Preview.

4. Go to **Slide 5**.

5. Insert a Click Box over the **New** command on the slide. The Click Box should take learners to the **next slide** if clicked.

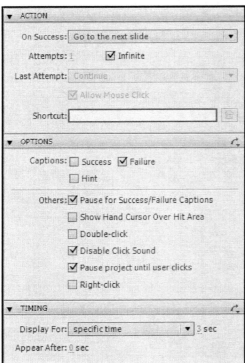

6. Edit the Failure Caption text so that it reads **Click here** (use Callout Type 5).

7. Position the Click Box over the New command and then resize the Click Box as necessary so it is no larger than the **New** command; position the Failure Caption in a similar position as shown in the picture below.

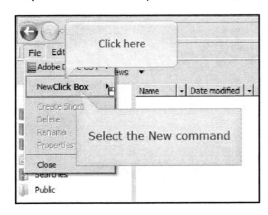

8. Insert similar Click Boxes on **Slides 6** and **8**.

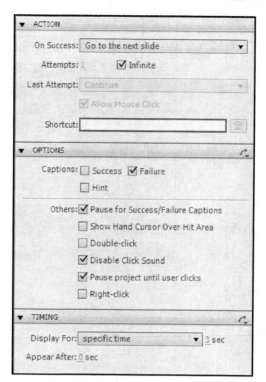

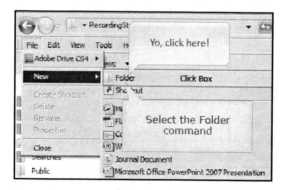

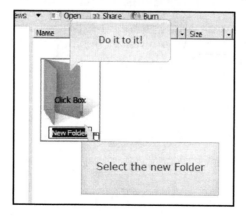

9. Preview the project and test each of the Click Boxes you added.

10. When finished, close the preview.

11. Save and close the project.

Text Entry Boxes

You can use Text Entry Boxes to simulate areas in an application that require a user to type data. You can instruct users to type specific information into a Text Entry Box and, depending on what they type, captions can provide the appropriate feedback.

Student Activity: Insert a Text Entry Box

1. Open **PasswordMe** from the Captivate5EssentialsData folder.

2. Edit the Style for new Text Entry Boxes.

   ❒ choose **Edit > Object Style Manager**

   ❒ from the Standard Objects group, select **Text Entry Box**

   ❒ at the right of the dialog box, change the Family to **Verdana**

   ❒ change the Size to **15**

   ❒ change the Transition to **No Transition**

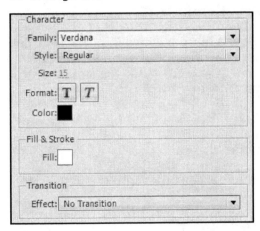

   ❒ click the **OK** button

3. Go to **Slide 1**.

   There is a transparent Text Caption on the slide instructing the learner to enter a password to take the course. You will create a Text Entry Box that will accept a specific password.

4. Insert a Text Entry Box.

   ❒ choose **Insert > Standard Objects > Text Entry Box**

   A couple of things happen on the slide. A small Text Entry Box has been added along, with some other objects. In the foreground, there is a Correct Entries box where you can specify the password you would like a learner to type.

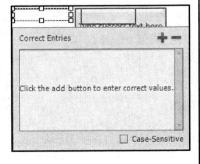

5. Add a Correct Entry.

❑ in the upper right of the Correct Entries window, click the **Plus** sign

❑ type **wordpass**

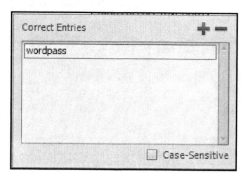

6. Set the General Properties for the Text Entry Box.

❑ with the Text Entry Box on Slide 1 selected, choose **Window > Properties**

❑ from the General group, deselect **Retain Text**

With this option deselected, the text a learner types into the Text Entry Box will be removed should the learner rewind and take the lesson again.

❑ if necessary, select **Show Text Box Frame**

This option will ensure that the Text Entry Box is visible to the learner.

❑ if necessary, select **Password Field**

With this option selected, the text a learner types into the Text Entry Box will be replaced by asterisks.

❑ if necessary, select **Validate User Input**

The text a learner types into the Text Entry Box will be checked against the Correct Entry you typed when you added the Text Entry Box.

❑ ensure that the remaining General properties match the image below

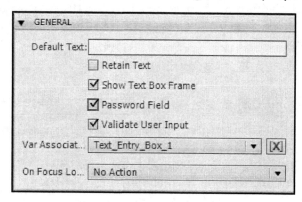

7. Set the Action for the Text Entry Box.

   ❏ from the Action group, On Success drop-down menu, select **Go to the next slide**

   ❏ ensure that the Attempts is set to **Infinite**

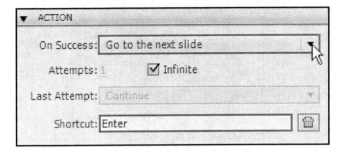

8. Set the Options for the Text Entry Box.

   ❏ from the Options group, Captions area, deselect both **Success** and **Hint**

   ❏ if necessary, select **Failure**

   ❏ ensure that the remaining options match the image below

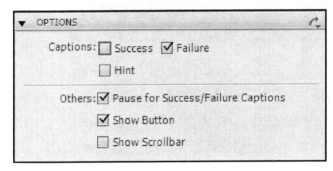

9. Save your work.

Confidence Check

1. Move/resize/edit the screen objects until the slide looks similar to image below.

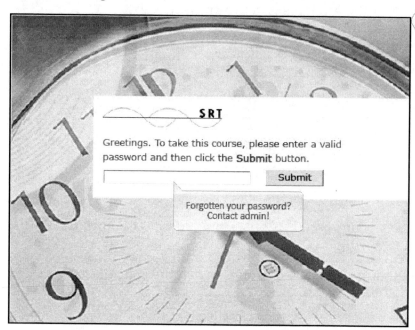

2. Preview the project.

3. Type **Hello** into the Text Entry Box and then click the **Submit** button.

    Because you did not type the text correctly, the Failure Caption appears.

4. Type **wordpass** into the box and then click the Submit button.

    This time the lesson continues without incident.

5. Close the preview.

6. Save and close the project.

iCONLOGiC
"Skills and Drills" Learning

Module 10: Introduction to Question Slides

In This Module You Will Learn About:

- Quiz Setup, page 164
- Add Question Slides, page 168

And You Will Learn To:

- Edit Quizzing Object Styles, page 164
- Set the Quiz Preferences, page 165
- Insert Question Slides, page 168
- Format a Question Slide, page 169
- Add an Image to a Question Slide, page 171
- Paste as Background, page 172

Quiz Setup

You will soon be adding a few question slides to your project. Before proceeding, it's a good idea to set up a few things first. For instance, if you set up the Object Styles for the Quiz objects, your question slides will look consistent. In addition, you should set up some basic Quiz Preferences to control such things as general navigation and the Pass/Fail options.

Student Activity: Edit Quizzing Object Styles

1. Open **QuizMe** from the Captivate5EssentialsData folder.

2. Use the Object Style Manager to set the formatting for Quizzing Objects.

   ❏ choose **Edit > Object Style Manager**

   ❏ at the upper left of the Object Style Manager dialog box, expand the **Quizzing Objects** group

   ❏ expand the **Captions** group

   ❏ select **Correct Caption** and, at the right side of the dialog box, change the Family to **Verdana**

   ❏ change the Size to **15**

   ❏ change the Transition Effect to **Fade In Only**

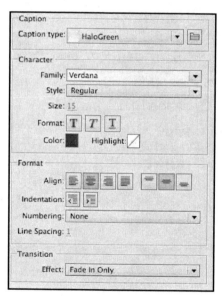

You have probably noticed that there are several Quizzing Objects. Each one would need your attention before you could get to the fun stuff and actually create a quiz. Never fear, I have already set the formats of the remaining objects for you so you won't have to.

3. Explore the Quizzing Objects styles.

   ❏ from the Quizzing Objects group, select any of the remaining objects and notice that the font has already been updated to Verdana and the size set to 15 for most of the objects

   ❏ click the **OK** button

Student Activity: Set the Quiz Preferences

1. The **QuizMe** project should still be open.

2. Go to Slide 10.

   You'll be adding a quiz after this slide.

3. Set the Quiz Preferences.

   ☐ choose **Quiz > Quiz Preferences**

   The Preferences dialog box opens with the Quiz > Reporting Category already selected.

   ☐ select **Settings** from the **Quiz** category

   ☐ from the **Quiz** area, change the Name of the Quiz to **Folders Quiz**

   ☐ from the Required drop-down menu, select **Answer All - The user must answer every question to continue**

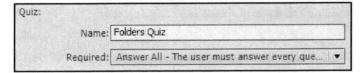

   ☐ from the **Settings** area, ensure your options match the picture below

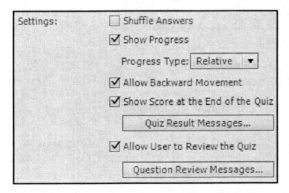

   If you had selected **Shuffle Answers**, the answers would appear in a different order on each Question Slide when users take the quiz. The **Show Progress** option will insert a counter on each Question Slide so that learners know where they are in the quiz. **Allow backward movement** will allow learners to go back and answer skipped questions. By selecting **Show score at end of quiz**, Captivate will add an additional slide at the end of the Question Slides that will summarize how the learner did on the quiz. The **Allow User to Review the Quiz** option will allow learners to go back and see how they answered the questions. However, once the answers are submitted for scoring, learners will not be able to change their answers.

4. Set the Pass or Fail options for the Quiz.

❑ from the **Quiz** Category, select **Pass or Fail**

❑ from the Pass/Fail options area, change the **% or more of total points to pass** to **50**

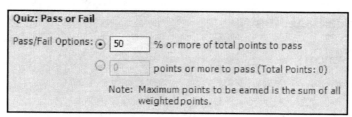

You are about to create a 2-question quiz. Your learners will now need to get at least 1 of the 2 questions correct to pass the quiz.

5. Set the Passing and Failing Grade action.

❑ from the Action drop-down menu for both If Passing Grade and If Failing Grade, choose **Go to the next slide**

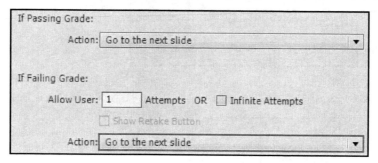

6. Review the Default question button labels.

❑ from the **Quiz** category, select **Default Labels**

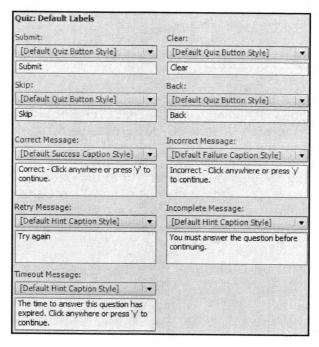

When your Question Slides are created, there will be buttons added automatically along the bottom of the slide allowing learners to submit their answers, clear selections, skip a question and go back and answer skipped questions. There will also be feedback captions learners will see as they get the answers correct or incorrect.

As you get more comfortable creating question slides in Captivate, feel free to return to this screen to make changes. For now, the defaults will work nicely.

❏ click the **OK** button

There should be a new slide in your project between—the Results slide that you specified when you enabled **Show score at end of quiz**. The other options you set will not be obvious. You will see those results as you insert Question Slides, which you will do next.

Note: The Results should be positioned after Slide 10... if not, please drag the Results slide after Slide 10 now.

7. Save your work.

Add Question Slides

You can create a self-scoring quiz without leaving Captivate. Each question you create appears on a new slide. The questions you create can be Multiple Choice, True/False, Fill-in-the-Blank, Short Answer, Matching, Hot Spot, Sequence or Rating Scale (Likert).

Student Activity: Insert Question Slides

1. The **QuizMe** project should still be open.

2. Insert a Multiple Choice and True/False Question Slide.

   ❑ select **Slide 10**

   ❑ choose **Quiz > Question Slide**

   The Insert Questions dialog box appears. If you were to click the Help link in the lower left of the dialog box, you could read more information about the available question types.

   ❑ select **Multiple Choice** and **True/False** from the list of Question Types

   ❑ ensure that 1 appears in the field to the right of each question type

   ❑ ensure that **Graded** is selected from the drop-down menu to the right of each Question type

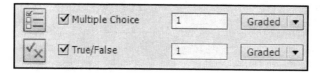

   ❑ click the **OK** button

   Two new slides are added to your project. One contains the Multiple Choice question; the other contains the True/False question.

3. Save your work.

Student Activity: Format a Question Slide

1. Type a Question and set a Point value.

   ☐ go to Slide 11

   ☐ triple-click the Type the question here text and replace it with **Folder names can contain how many characters?**

   ☐ deselect the text box and then resize it so that it is wide enough to display the text you just typed

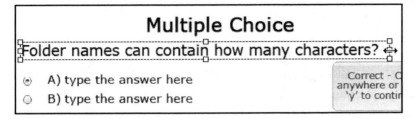

2. Type two of the Answers.

   ☐ replace the first "type the answer here" with **9**

   ☐ replace the second "type the answer here" with **255**

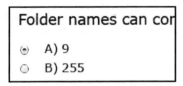

3. Add two more answers and change the point value for the question.

   ☐ double-click the middle of Slide 11 to display the Quiz Properties for the question

   ☐ from the General group, change the **Answers** to **4**

   ☐ change the Points to **1**

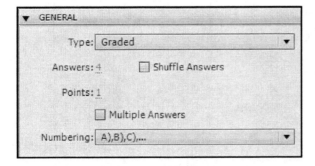

   In addition to the question now being worth just a single point, two more answers have been added to the slide.

4. Replace the third "type the answer here" with **8.**

5. Replace the last "type the answer here" with **256.**

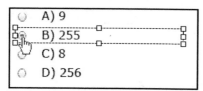

A) 9
B) 255
C) 8
D) 256

6. Specify one of the answers as the correct answer.

☐ click in the circle to the left of **B) 255**

A) 9
B) 255
C) 8
D) 256

Your question slide should look like this:

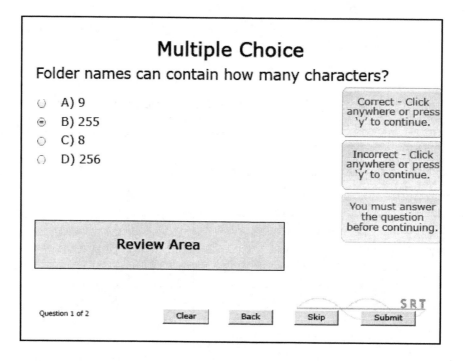

Multiple Choice
Folder names can contain how many characters?

A) 9
B) 255
C) 8
D) 256

Correct - Click anywhere or press 'y' to continue.

Incorrect - Click anywhere or press 'y' to continue.

You must answer the question before continuing.

Review Area

Question 1 of 2   Clear   Back   Skip   Submit

7. Save your work.

Student Activity: Add an Image to a Question Slide

1. The **QuizMe** project should still be open.

2. Insert an image.

   ❏ ensure that you are on **Slide 11** and then choose **Insert > Image**

   ❏ from the **Captivate5EssentialsData\images_animation** folder, open **pop_quiz.jpg**

3. Change the image's slide position.

   ❏ display the Properties panel for the image

   ❏ on the Position & Size panel, change the X and Y values to **0**

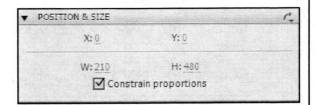

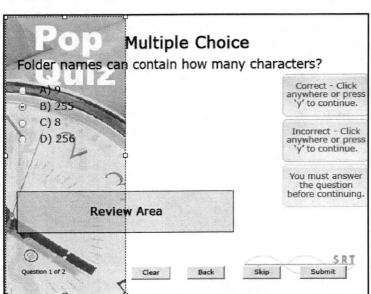

4. Merge the image into the slide's background.

   ❏ on the Timeline, right-click the **pop_quiz** object and choose **Merge with the background**

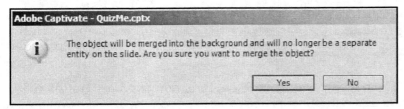

   ❏ click the **Yes** button

   With the image merged into the background, the slide and the image you inserted are now one entity. This will prove very useful in the next activity.

Student Activity: Paste as Background

1. The **QuizMe** project should still be open.

2. Copy a slide's background.

   ☐ right-click **Slide 11** and choose **Copy Background**

3. Paste as Background.

   ☐ go to **Slide 12**

   Notice that this slide does not yet have the same background image as Slide 11.

   ☐ right-click **Slide 12** and choose **Paste as Background**

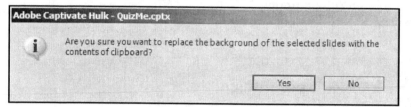

   ☐ click the **Yes** button

   ☐ right-click **Slide 13** (the results slide) and choose **Paste as Background**

   ☐ click the **Yes** button

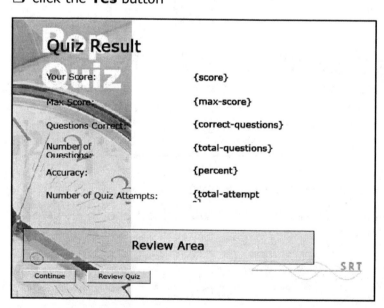

Cool stuff! The background from Slide 11 is now the background for Slides 12 and 13. Without this slick Captivate shortcut, you would have had to insert the pop_quiz image onto each slide, move it to the far left of each slide and then merge the image into the background. You can use this technique to apply the background of any slide to the background of another slide (or multiple slides).

4. Save your work.

Confidence Check

1. The QuizMe project should still be open.

2. Move/resize the Slide 11 objects as necessary so that the slide looks similar to the image below.

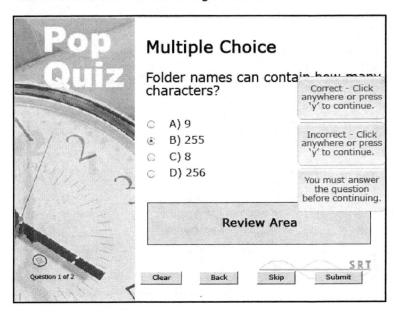

3. Edit and then move/resize the Slide 12 objects as necessary so that the slide looks similar to the image below.

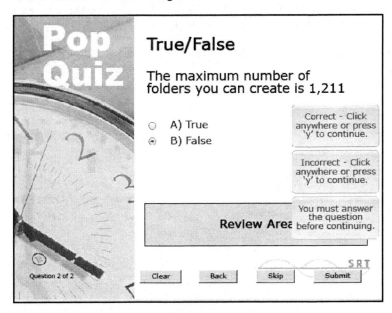

4. Change the Point value for Slide 12 to 1 point (you learned how on page 169).

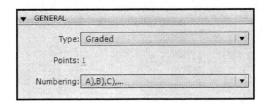

5. Move/resize the Slide 13 objects as necessary so that the slide looks similar to the image below.

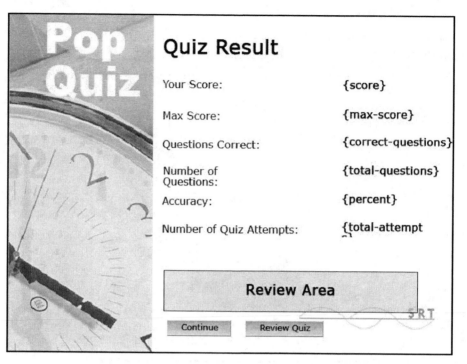

6. Preview the project and take the quiz. (Hopefully you will receive a passing score.)

7. When finished, close the preview. If not happy with the appearance of either of the question slides or the results slide, make any changes as you see fit.

8. Save and close the project.

iCONLOGiC

"Skills and Drills" Learning

Module 11: Publishing

In This Module You Will Learn About:

- URL Actions, page 176
- Skins, page 179
- Table of Contents, page 183
- Preloaders, page 185
- Publishing, page 187
- Round Tripping, page 192

And You Will Learn To:

- Link to a Web Site, page 176
- Apply a Skin, page 179
- Edit and Save a Skin, page 180
- Delete a Skin, page 181
- Create a TOC, page 183
- Add a Loading Screen, page 185
- Publish a Flash (SWF), page 187
- Publish Word Handouts, page 190
- Export Captions, page 192
- Perform a "Round Trip", page 194

URL Actions

You learned how to use Click Boxes on page 152 to add interactivity to your projects. But you can use Click Boxes for other purposes. For instance, a Click Box can be used to link an area of a slide to a Web site or other remote file. You can use a Click Box to create an e-mail link. And you can use Click Boxes to create links between your projects. You'll learn how to perform all of these actions during the next few activities.

Student Activity: Link to a Web Site

1. Open PublishMe from the Captivate5EssentialsData folder.

2. Insert a Click Box.

   ☐ go to **Slide 4**

   There is a picture of SRT's home page on the slide. You are going to attach a URL to a Click Box that will open the SRT home page in a Web browser.

   ☐ choose **Insert > Standard Objects > Click Box**

   A Click Box and three captions are added to the slide.

3. Set the On Success action for the Click Box to open a Web page.

   ☐ double-click the Click Box to display the **Properties** panel

   ☐ from the **Action** group, On Success drop-down menu, select **Open URL or file**

   ☐ type **http://www.southrivertechnologies.com** into the URL field

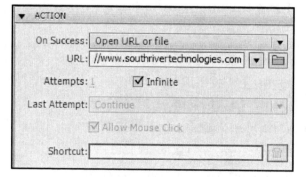

4. Force the browser window to appear in a new window and stop the lesson from continuing to play.

   ☐ click the black triangle to the right of the URL you just typed and choose **New**

   This option will force the link into a new browser window instead of replacing your lesson with the Web site.

   ☐ deselect **Continue playing project**

With this option deselected, there is no chance that the lesson will continue to play while the SRT Web page is covering the lesson.

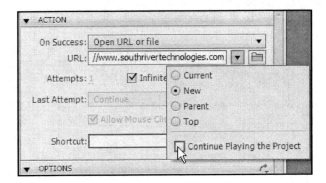

5. Set the Click Box options.

   ❏ with the Properties panel for the Click Box still open, move to the Options group and from the Captions area, deselect **Success**, **Failure** and **Hint**

   The Click Box you added is something that *must* be clicked by a learner so there is no need to include the Captions.

   ❏ from the Others area, select **Show Hand Cursor Over Hit Area**

   By enabling this option, learners who move to click the Click Box will see a Hand Cursor, a universal sign that the Click Box will take them someplace (typically another slide or a Web site).

   ❏ ensure the only other selected option is **Pause project until user clicks**

   Without this option, the lesson would end before a learner had a chance to click the Click Box.

6. Resize the Click Box.

   ❏ resize the Click Box as necessary so that it covers the Web site graphic

7. Save your work.

Confidence Check

1. Still working on Slide 4 of the PublishMe project, **Copy** the Click Box (**Edit > Copy**) and **Paste** it (**Edit > Paste**) onto the slide.

2. Drag the new Click Box so it covers the envelope graphic and resize the Click Box so that it is the same size as the e-mail area of the image.

3. Show the Properties of the new Click Box and, on the Action group, select **Send e-mail to** from the **On Success** drop-down menu.

4. Type **your e-mail address** into the **Address** field.

5. Preview the project.

6. Test the URL link. You will not be able to test the e-mail link unless you are working from your own computer and an e-mail client (such as Outlook) has been installed and set up on your computer.

7. When finished, close the browser window and close the Preview.

Skins

Skins perform much the same function in a project as your clothes perform for you. Visit top websites during the holidays (**amazon.com**, **google.com**, etc.) and you'll see that the "skin" used on the site reflects the season. Bored during the day? Maybe changing your clothes would be enough to change your attitude. And Skins can be customized to suit your taste—you can select from myriad playbars, buttons and color schemes.

Student Activity: Apply a Skin

1. The PublishMe project should still be open.

2. Preview the project (**File > Preview**) and notice that there is a playbar at the bottom of the lesson window. The playbar is one component of a Skin.

3. Close the preview.

4. Apply a skin to the project.

   ❑ choose **Window > Skin Editor**

   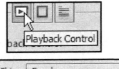

   ❑ if necessary, select the **Playback Control** button

   ❑ from the Skin drop-down menu, choose **Pearls**

   Observe the preview. Among other things, notice the color of the playbar, its position on the slide, and that Closed Captioning and Mute are both selected from the list of options at the left.

5. Close the Skin window and then preview the Project. Notice the Pearls skin has been applied to the lesson. When finished, close the preview.

Student Activity: Edit and Save a Skin

1. The PublishMe project should still be open.

2. Remove an unnecessary control from the playbar.

   ☐ choose **Window > Skin Editor**

   ☐ if necessary, select **Pearls** from the Skin drop-down menu

   ☐ from the lower left of the Skin Editor window, remove the check mark from **Closed Captioning**

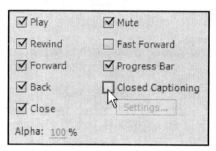

   This project does not have any closed captions so this option is truly unnecessary.

3. Save the modifications to the skin.

   ☐ click the **Save As** button 💾

   ☐ change the name to **Pearls_NoCC**

   ☐ click the **OK** button

4. Apply a different skin.

   ☐ select **DarkChocolate** 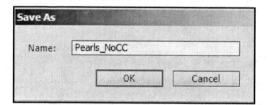 from the Skin drop-down menu

   Notice on the preview that the color of your playbar changes to reflect the new skin.

5. Reapply the edited Pearls skin.

   ☐ select **Pearls_NoCC** from the Skin drop-down menu

Student Activity: Delete a Skin

1. The PublishMe project should still be open along with the Skin Editor window.

2. Delete a skin.

   ☐ ensure that **Pearls_NoCC** is the selected Skin

   ☐ click the **Delete** button 🗑

3. Apply a different skin, edit it and then save it.

   ☐ select **SpaceBlue** from the Skin list

   ☐ remove the check mark from **Closed Captioning**

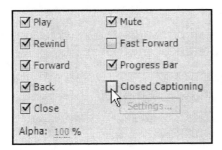

   ☐ click the **Save As** button 💾

   ☐ name the skin **SpaceBlue_NoCC**

   ☐ click the **OK** button

Confidence Check

1. Spend a few moments applying some of the other skins to your project.

2. After you have settled on your favorite skin, preview the project to ensure the skin still meets with your approval.

3. Edit the skin so that it does not use the Closed Caption option.

4. Save the edited skin with a name that reflects the missing Closed Captioning (such as **name_NoCC**).

5. Close the Skin Editor window.

6. Choose **File > Project Info**.

7. Fill in the information with your personal information (the information that you type here will appear on the TOC you are about to create).

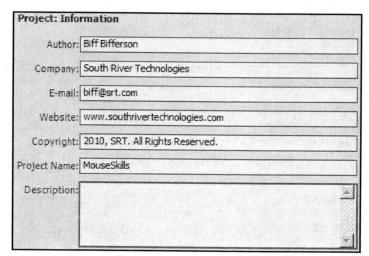

8. Click OK and then save your work.

Table of Contents

You can create a TOC that will serve as a nice navigation vehicle for your users. By simply selecting **Show TOC** on the TOC tab of the Skin Editor, you are creating a nice menu system for your users (without the need to take the project into Flash).

Student Activity: Create a TOC

1. The PublishMe project should still be open.

2. Show and populate the TOC.

   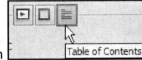

   ☐ choose **Window > Skin Editor**

   ☐ click the Table of Contents button

   ☐ select **Show TOC**

   By simply selecting Show TOC, an empty TOC has been added to the left of the lesson. Next you will add the four slides in the lesson to the TOC.

   ☐ add check marks to all four slides

   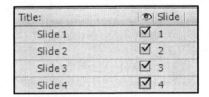

3. Title the slides on the TOC.

   ☐ double-click the current Title for Slide 1

   ☐ replace the current title with the word **Home**

4. Close the Skin Editor window.

5. Save your work.

Confidence Check

1. Still working in the PublishMe project, reopen the Skin Editor window.

2. Change the titles of the remaining slides to match the image below.

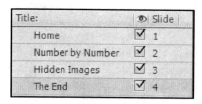

3. Close the Skin Editor window.

4. Preview the project and notice that your TOC (also known as a menu) appears at the left of your lesson).

5. As you move through the lesson, green check marks are automatically added to the TOC. Nice!

6. Close the preview.

7. Open the Skin Editor window, click the Table of Contents button and click the **Info** button at the bottom of the window.

8. It appears that the project information you added back on page 182 isn't here. Or is it? Click the **Project Information** button and the fields in the TOC information field will be filled with the project information you added earlier.

9. In the Photo area, click the Browse button. 🗀

10. Click the **Import** button.

11. From the Captivate5EssentialsData/ images_animation folder, open **biff_baby.jpg**.

12. Click the **OK** button to close the TOC Information dialog box.

13. Notice that the information and photo appear in the upper left of the TOC.

14. Close the Skin Editor window and save your work.

Preloaders

If your learners are using a slow Internet connection and your lesson is large (over 10-15 megabytes) it will take a significant amount of time for the lesson to begin playing on the learner's computer. Since most people will not wait for more than a few seconds for something to happen on their computer before giving up, a loading screen—an image or message that appears during those first critical seconds while the first part of the project is downloading— is important.

Student Activity: Add a Loading Screen

1. The PublishMe project should still be open.

2. Confirm the Publish Settings.

   ❐ choose **File > Publish Settings**

   ❐ ensure that your Settings match the picture below (all are Captivate defaults)

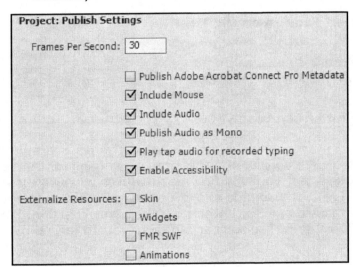

Most of the Publish Settings options are self-explanatory. However, **Externalize Resources** bears some additional explanation. Your goal when publishing your content is to keep the number of published files to a minimum to make file management and uploads to Web servers as simple as possible. By default, resources such as Skins and Animations are published within the lesson. This will result is a larger SWF when you publish. Unless your SWFs are very large, consider leaving the options as shown above.

3. Add a loading screen.

   ❐ from the Project category, select **Start and End**

   ❐ ensure **Auto Play** is selected from the **Project start options** area

   With Auto Play selected, the lesson will being playing as soon as it is downloaded.

   ❐ select **Preloader**

   ❐ click the **Browse** button to the right of Preloader

You should automatically be browsing the Preloaders folder.

❑ from the AS3 folder (AS3 stands for ActionScript 3), open **DefaultPreloader.swf**

4. Set a Preloader %.

❑ change the Preloader % to **50**

The Preloader % is the percentage of the published Captivate SWF file that must be downloaded before the lesson begins to play on the learner's computer.

5. Set the project fade options.

❑ if necessary, select **Fade In on the First Slide**

❑ ensure **Stop project** is selected from the Action drop-down menu in the Project End Options area

❑ deselect **Fade Out on the Last Slide**

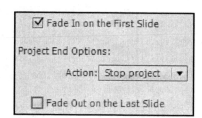

Fading in on the first slide is a nice effect. However, I've discovered that fading out on the last slide doesn't offer near the same bang for the buck. In fact, if you leave it selected, you may find that it causes other problems with items on your Timeline that also fade in and/or out, or objects that pause the slide action. As for the Action area, I prefer the Stop Project action. When the lesson is finished, it will stop. The learner can then elect to rewind the lesson or close the lesson.

❑ click the **OK** button

6. Save your work.

Publishing

Publishing in Captivate takes your source content and outputs it into a format that can be viewed by the user. The most common way to publish a Captivate project is as a Flash SWF—an ideal solution for Web deployment since the resulting SWF files can be viewed by the vast majority of the world's browsers and operating systems. Your users will not need Captivate installed on their computer to view a published SWF, but they will need the free Adobe Flash Player (**http://www.adobe.com**). The Flash Player is installed on most computers in use today.

If you are concerned with users not having the Flash Player, consider publishing a Standalone project instead of a SWF. This kind of output is a self-contained, self-running file that includes the Flash Player. There are Standalone outputs for both the Macintosh and PC.

Student Activity: Publish a Flash (SWF)

1. The PublishMe project should still be open.

2. Specify a Publish format and Project Title.

   ❏ choose **File > Publish**

   The Publish dialog box opens.

   ❏ select **Flash (SWF)** from the list at the left

   ❏ confirm that the Project Title is **MouseSkills**

   The Project Title will end up being the physical names of the files you publish. Because your published files will likely be stored on a Web server, you should not use spaces in Project Titles.

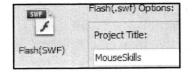

3. Select a Publish folder.

   ❏ click the **Browse** button

   ❏ navigate to **Captivate5EssentialsData\published_projects**

   ❏ click the **OK** button (Mac users, click the **Choose** button)

   ❏ if necessary, select **Publish to Folder**

   The **Publish to Folder** option will create a folder inside the published_projects folder called MouseSkills. There will be occasions when you will not want to create a new folder when publishing—a decision you will have to make on a project-by-project basis.

4. Select the Output Options.

❏ from the Output Options area, select **Export To HTML**

❏ deselect the other Output options

You typically only need to select Zip Files if you intend to upload your project to a Learning Management System (LMS) as a content package. And Fullscreen would cause your project to take over the learner's entire screen, something that most learners would not appreciate.

❏ from the Flash Player Version drop-down menu, select **Flash Player 9**

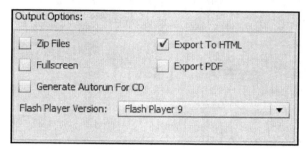

At the time this book was printed, Flash Player 10 was the latest and greatest version of the Flash Player and has been in circulation for more than a year. However, if you were to select a Flash Player version that's too new, learners who have an older version of the Flash Player would be unable to watch your published lesson. By selecting Flash Player 9, you are almost guaranteeing that your lesson will play on most PCs and Macs around the world.

5. Publish the lesson.

❏ click the **Publish** button

Captivate creates a folder inside the published_projects folder that contains all of the published files. You are then prompted to view the output.

❏ click the **Yes** button

The lesson opens in your default Web browser.

When you published the lesson, Captivate published two main files: the Small Web Format (SWF) and an HTML file. There is also a JavaScript file (standard.js) that will ensure that your lesson will play correctly in a Web browser. If the HTML file is opened by a Web browser, code within the HTML page loads into the browser and immediately looks for the JavaScript file. Assuming the JavaScript file is found, more data is added into the HTML page that will instruct the SWF file to play within the Web browser. *These published files should always be kept together.*

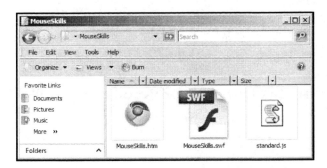

6. Close the Web browser and return to Captivate.

Confidence Check

1. Display the Publish dialog box.

2. From the Publish options at the left, select **Media**.

3. If you are on a PC, choose **Windows Executable** as the Media type; if you are on a Mac, choose **MAC Executable** as the Media type

4. Ensure that the publish Folder is **Captivate5 EssentialsData\published_projects\ MouseSkills**.

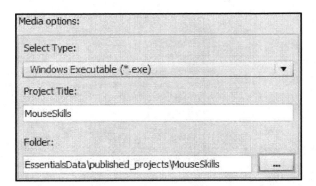

5. Publish and then View the Output.

6. Return to Captivate.

Student Activity: Publish Word Handouts

1. The PublishMe project should still be open.

2. Publish the project as Word Handouts.

   ❏ choose **File > Publish**

   The Publish Options appear.

   ❏ from the left side of the dialog box, select **Print**

   ❏ the Project Title should still be **MouseSkills**

   ❏ ensure that the publish Folder is still
   Captivate5EssentialsData\published_projects\MouseSkills

   ❏ ensure that the Export range is set to **All**

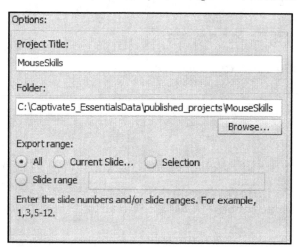

   ❏ from the Type drop-down menu, select **Handouts**

3. Set the layout options.

   ❏ from the **Handout Layout Options** area, ensure that **Use table in the output** is selected

   ❏ change the **Slides per page** to **3**

   ❏ select **Caption Text**

   ❏ select **Add blank line for notes**

   ❏ select **Include objects and questions**

   ❏ the four remaining options should be deselected

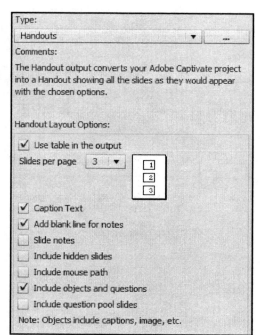

4. Publish the document.

   ❏ click the **Publish** button

   When the project has been published, a dialog box will give you an attempt to View the Output.

   ❏ click the **Yes** button

   The handout opens in Microsoft Word. Since you selected 3 slides per page, Caption text, and Blank lines, the slide images are very small.

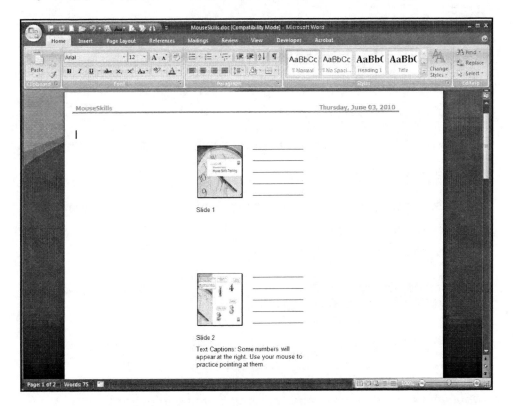

5. Close the Word document, and return to Captivate.

Round Tripping

Exporting captions to Microsoft Word is one of my favorite Captivate features. Why? If you export the captions to Word, any team member can open the exported document with Word and make editorial changes. Those changes can be *imported back into Captivate*—something I call **Round Tripping**.

You can use this round-trip workflow to create multiple-language versions of your project without having to rerecord or recreate the project. All you would have to do is send the exported captions to an interpreter and have the caption text translated into another language. You would then import the translated captions back into your project. *Cool!*

Student Activity: Export Captions

1. The PublishMe project should still be open.

2. Export the project captions.

   ❏ choose **File > Export > Project Captions and Closed Captions**

   The Save As dialog box appears.

   ❏ ensure that you are saving to the Captivate5EssentialsData folder
   ❏ click the **Save** button

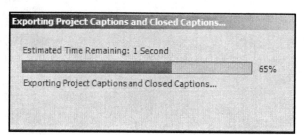

You will be notified when the captions have been exported.

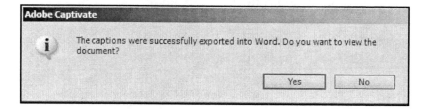

   ❏ click the **Yes** button to open the Word document

The captions have been imported into a Word table. There are five columns with the following headers: **Slide ID**, **Item ID**, **Original Text Caption Data**, **Updated Text Caption Data** and **Slide**. You can make any changes you want to the Updated Text Caption Data, but do not change any of the other information. The Slide ID identifies which slide your edited captions go to. The Item ID identifies which caption goes with which caption data.

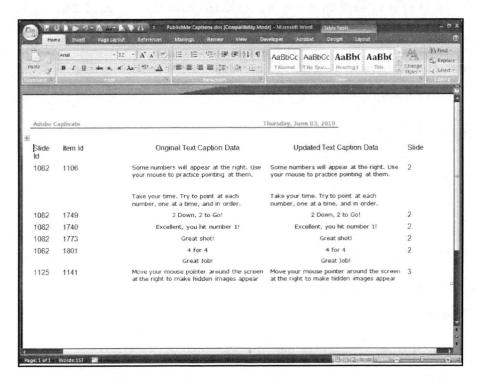

3. Update the Word content.

   ❏ on Slide ID **1125**, Item ID **1141**, find the phrase **Move your mouse pointer around the screen at the right to make hidden images appear** in the **Updated Text Caption Data** column

   ❏ change the text to **If you like surprises, move your mouse pointer around the screen and hidden images will appear**

1082	1801	4 for 4	4 for 4	2
		Great Job!	Great Job!	
1125	1141	Move your mouse pointer around the screen at the right to make hidden images appear	If you like surprises, move your mouse pointer around the screen and hidden images will appear	3

4. Save the Word document and exit Word.

5. Return to Captivate.

Student Activity: Perform a "Round Trip"

1. The PublishMe project should still be open.

2. Import the edited caption back into the Captivate project.

   ❑ choose **File > Import > Project Captions and Closed Captions**

   The Open dialog box appears.

   ❑ open **PublishMe Captions** from the Captivate5EssentialsData folder

   You will be notified that the items were imported into the project.

   ❑ click the **OK** button

3. Review the updated caption.

   ❑ go to **Slide 3**

   Notice that the text you changed in the Word document has been updated on the slide.

   > If you like surprises, move your mouse pointer around the screen and hidden images will appear

4. Save your work and close the project.

Want to Learn More About Adobe Captivate?

Congratulations! By completing the lessons in this book, you have learned the essential skills that will enable you to immediately create effective demonstrations and simulations in Adobe Captivate.

But you're not finished with your Captivate learning journey. If you'd like to go beyond the basics and learn even more about Captivate, consider our *Adobe Captivate 5: Beyond the Essentials* book.

Topics covered in the *Adobe Captivate 5: Beyond the Essentials* book include, but are not limited to:

- ❑ Project Templates
- ❑ Master Slides
- ❑ Custom Object Styles
- ❑ PowerPoint Round-Trip Workflow
- ❑ Project Import/Branching
- ❑ Quiz Pools
- ❑ Collaborating
- ❑ Widgets
- ❑ Variables
- ❑ Aggregator Projects
- ❑ Advanced Actions
- ❑ LMS and Acrobat.com Integration

If you would like to learn more about *Adobe Captivate 5: Beyond the Essentials*, visit **http://www.iconlogic.com**.

iCONLOGiC

"Skills and Drills" Learning

Appendix: FMRs, Panning, Manual Mode & Slideshows

In This Module You Will Learn About:

- Full Motion Recording, page 198
- Panning, page 202
- Manual Mode, page 206
- Image Slideshows, page 208

And You Will Learn To:

- Create an FMR, page 198
- Record a Lesson With Panning, page 202
- Record Manually, page 206
- Create an Image Slideshow, page 208

Full Motion Recording

When you record screen actions using Captivate's automatic modes (Demonstration or one of the Simulations), clicking your mouse or pressing [Print Screen] on your keyboard (or whatever key you set up) results in a screen capture. However, if you need to capture complex procedures like drawing, moving or resizing an object, you can use Full Motion Recording (FMR). Assuming you have not disabled the FMR mode, and that you are recording a lesson in an automatic recording mode, all you need to do to create an FMR is drag your mouse during the recording process. When you finish the recording process, any slides containing FMR videos will contain a movie camera icon when viewed on the Edit tab. The FMR will play like an animation within your project—a movie within a movie.

Student Activity: Create an FMR

1. Captivate should be running (no projects should be open).

2. Set Captivate's FMR Preferences.

   ☐ if you are using a PC, choose **Edit > Preferences**;
   if you are using a Mac, choose **Adobe Captivate > Preferences**

   ☐ from the Recording category, select **Settings**

   ☐ from the **Automatically use FMR for** area at the bottom of the dialog box, select **Drag and Drop actions** and **Mouse Wheel Actions**

By selecting Drag and Drop actions, dragging your mouse during the recording process will result in an automatic FMR video being recorded for you. In addition, scrolling by using 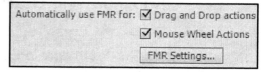 the mouse wheel (if your mouse supports this feature) will automatically result in an FMR.

   ☐ click the **FMR Settings** button

The Full Motion Recording preferences appear.

   ☐ ensure that your options match the picture below (with the exception of the Working Folder... the information here will vary from computer to computer)

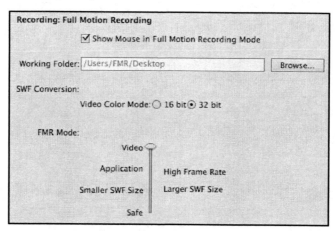

By selecting **Show Mouse in Full Motion Recording Mode**, the video you record will include a mouse pointer in the Full Motion Recording.

The **SWF Conversion** was set to **32 bit**. Most computers have video set to 32 bit, which offers the widest range of colors on the monitor. If you were to select 16 bit, you would end up with a smaller FMR, but a smaller range of colors—and a lower-quality video.

The **FMR Mode** in the previous picture was set to **Video**, which will result in the highest-quality SWF you can get from your FMR (and the largest file size). You could elect to use **Application** or **Smaller SWF Size**, both of which would result in a lower-quality FMR and SWF. When in doubt, you could use **Safe** mode and Captivate would calculate your available system resources and create the best possible FMR.

❐ click the **OK** button

3. Rehearse the lesson you are going to record.

   ❐ minimize Captivate and start a Web browser

   ❐ using the browser, go to **http://www.disney.com**

   Like many commercial Web sites, this page is very long. You will not be able to use Captivate or any screen capture utility to capture the entire page. As a result, you will record a video using Captivate that demonstrates using the scroll bar to scroll down a Web page.

   ❐ at the right side of the browser window, drag the scroll bar **down** an inch or two to scroll down the Web page

   ❐ release your mouse

   ❐ drag the scroll bar **down** another inch or so to scroll further down the Web page

   ❐ release your mouse

   ❐ drag the scroll bar **down** another inch or so to scroll a bit further down the Web page

4. Reset the stage.

   ❐ scroll back to the top of the Web page

5. Display the recording control panel.

   ❐ switch back to Captivate

   ❐ from the Create New area of the Welcome Screen, click **Software Simulation**

   The Recording Area and control panel appear.

6. Select the browser window as the Application.

   ❑ from the top of the control panel, select **Application** (if necessary)

   ❑ from the drop-down menu that appears beneath Application, select the browser window

7. Specify a recording size.

   ❑ from the Snap to area, select **Custom Size** (if necessary)

   ❑ from the next drop-down menu, select **640 x 480** (if necessary)

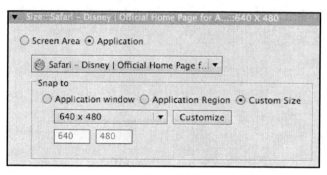

8. Select a Recording Mode.

   ❑ from the Recording Type area of the Control panel, select **Automatic** (if necessary)

   ❑ select **Demo** from the list of modes and deselect the remaining three modes

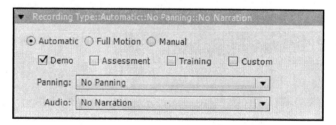

9. Disable Panning and Audio Narration.

   ❑ ensure that Panning is set to **No Panning** and that Audio is set to **No Narration**

10. Record the Demo.

    ❑ click the **Record** button

    ❑ at the right side of the browser window, drag the scroll bar **down** an inch or two to scroll down the Web page

    ❑ release your mouse

    ❑ drag the scroll bar **down** another inch or so to scroll further down the Web page

    ❑ release your mouse

    ❑ drag the scroll bar **down** another inch or so to scroll a bit further down the Web page

11. Stop the recording process.

❑ press [**End**] on your keyboard (or press whatever Stop Recording key you set up on page 27)

Note: If you can't get Captivate to stop recording via your keyboard shortcut, you can always manually stop the recording process by clicking the Captivate icon in the System Tray (PC users) or the Dock (Mac users).

12. Once the video opens within Captivate, notice that some of your slides contain a movie camera icon—these slides contain the FMR videos.

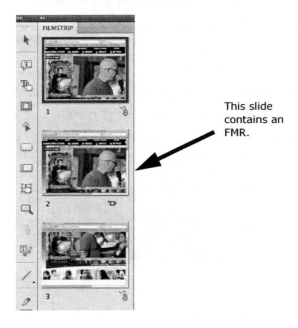

This slide contains an FMR.

13. Save the new project to the **Captivate5EssentialsData** folder as **ExampleOfFMR**.

14. Preview the project (**File > Preview**).

As you watch the preview, you will notice the FMR videos show the process of using the scroll bar.

15. When finished previewing the lesson, close the preview.

16. Save and then close the project.

Panning

Captivate's Panning feature is useful when you want to record something on your computer that is outside of the capture area. If you enable Panning prior to recording and use its Automatic mode, clicking outside of the capture area will force Captivate to move the recording area to include the area you clicked.

During the activity that follows, you will use the Panning feature to capture an area of the Walt Disney website that is outside the 640x480 capture area you have used so far.

Student Activity: Record a Lesson With Panning

1. Captivate should be running (no projects should be open).

2. Rehearse the lesson you are going to record.

   ❑ minimize Captivate and return to the Disney web site: **www.disney.com**

   ❑ resize the browser window so it's about 30 percent larger

   ❑ click on some of the links on the navigation bar (including one or two that are farther to the right of the resized window)

3. Reset the stage.

   ❑ return to the Disney web site: **www.disney.com**

4. Display the recording control panel.

   ❑ switch back to Captivate

   ❑ from the Create New area of the Welcome Screen, click **Software Simulation**

   The Recording Area and control panel appear.

5. Select a screen area to record instead of an application.

   ❑ from the top of the control panel, select **Screen Area**

6. Specify a recording size.

   ❏ from the Set Capture Area to area, select **Custom Size** (if necessary)

   ❏ from the next drop-down menu, select **640 x 480** (if necessary)

7. Drag the red recording box to the **upper left** of the browser window.

8. If necessary, resize the browser window so it's about 30 percent larger than the red Recording Area.

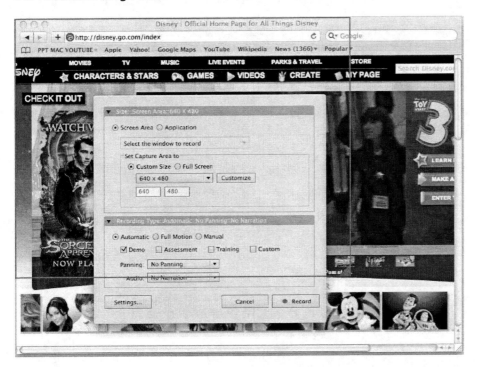

Because you selected Screen Area instead of Application, the Recording Area stays sized to 640 x 480 and does not get larger as you resize the browser window.

9. Select a Recording Mode.

   ❏ from the Recording Type area of the Control panel, select **Automatic** (if necessary)

   ❏ select **Demo** from the list of modes and deselect the remaining three modes

10. Enable Panning.

    ❏ from the Panning drop-down menu, select **Manual Panning**

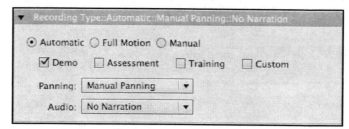

11. Record the Demo.

    ❏ click the **Record** button

    ❏ click on one or two of the links on the navigation bar (within the red Recording Area)

12. Manually pan.

    ❏ drag the right edge of the red Recording Area to the right so some of the navigation bar links at the right of the Web page are within the Recording Area

    ❏ click on one or two of the links on the navigation bar

13. Stop the recording process.

14. Preview the project (**File > Preview**).

15. When finished previewing the project, close the preview.

16. Save the new project to the **Captivate5EssentialsData** folder as **ExampleOfPanning**.

17. Close the project.

Manual Mode

If you've stepped through all of the modules in this book and the activities in this Appendix, you've now used just about every available recording option in Captivate except one—Manual mode. In most instances, the Automatic or Full Motion Recording Types will work just fine. However, you will come across some applications where neither of the Recording Types will work (some web applications are simply difficult to record). This is a perfect opportunity to use Captivate's Manual mode.

Student Activity: Record Manually

1. Captivate should be running (no projects should be open).

2. Rehearse the lesson you are going to record.

   ❑ minimize Captivate and return to the Disney web site: **www.disney.com**

   ❑ point, but don't click on some of the buttons in the site's navigation bar

   You'd like to capture the process of pointing to links, but recording the action with Captivate is going to be difficult because it takes mouse clicks to create screen captures.

3. Display the recording control panel.

   ❑ switch back to Captivate

   ❑ record a new **Software Simulation** (File menu)

   The Recording Area and control panel appear.

4. Select a screen area to record instead of an application.

   ❑ from the top of the control panel, select **Screen Area**

   ❑ select the Disney site from the drop-down menu

   ❑ from the Snap to area, select Custom Size

   ❑ from the next drop-down menu, select **640 x 480** (if necessary)

5. Select the Manual Recording Type.

   ❏ from the Recording Type area of the Control panel, select **Manual**

   ❏ change the Panning to **No Panning**

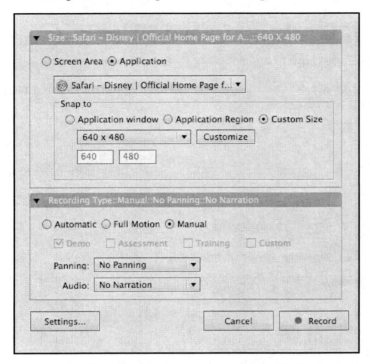

6. Record the Manual Demo.

   ❏ click the **Record** button

   Unlike the other modes, no screen capture is created for you. You'll need to create every screen capture on your own.

   ❏ PC users, press [**Print Screen**] on your keyboard; Mac users, press [**Command**] [**F6**]

   ❏ point to one of the links on the navigation bar

   ❏ PC users, press [**Print Screen**] on your keyboard; Mac users, press [**Command**] [**F6**]

   ❏ point to one of the links on the navigation bar

   ❏ PC users, press [**Print Screen**] on your keyboard; Mac users, press [**Command**] [**F6**]

7. Stop the recording.

8. Preview the project and notice that the screens you captured appear. But this is a bare-bones recording. You would now need to move through the project and add required project assets that recording in the Automatic mode would have included.

9. Close the project (there is no need to save it).

Image Slideshows

If you have a collection of images laying around your hard drive or server, you can use Captivate's Image Slideshow feature to quickly create a slideshow.

Student Activity: Create an Image Slideshow

1. Create an Image Slideshow project.

    ☐ from within Captivate, click **Image Slideshow** from the **Create New** area of the Welcome Screen

    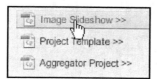

    The New Image Slideshow dialog box appears.

    ☐ from the **Select** drop-down menu, select **640 x 480**

    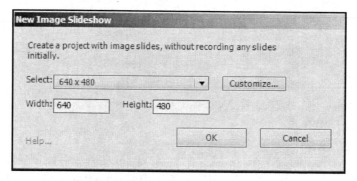

    ☐ click the **OK** button

2. Find the images to be used in the slideshow.

    ☐ navigate to **Captivate5EssentialsData**
    ☐ open the **images_animation** folder
    ☐ open the **SlideShowPictures** folder

    There are 15 images within the folder. You will be using all of the images in the slideshow.

    ☐ select **all** of the images in the folder
    ☐ click the **Open** button

    The Resize/Crop Image dialog box appears.

3. Set the Resize/Crop Image properties.

☐ select **Fit to Stage** from the options at the right of the dialog box (if necessary) and then click the **Apply to All** button

☐ click the **OK** button

The image slides are imported into a new project.

4. Save the project as **MySlideShow**.

Confidence Check

1. Preview the project.

2. Notice that the slideshow works, the photos are wonderful, but the slides move along just a bit too quickly.

3. Close the preview.

4. On the Filmstrip, select any slide.

5. Choose Edit > Select All to select all of the slides.

6. Choose **Window > Properties** to display the **Properties** panel.

7. Scroll down and notice that the Display Time for the selected slides is 3.0 seconds.

8. Change the Display Time to **5** seconds.

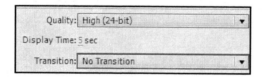

9. Preview the project.

   The timing is better. But wouldn't it be even better if there was a transition between one slide and the next? You bet...

10. Double-click the first slide in the project to display the **Properties** panel.

11. From the **Transition** drop-down menu, select any Transition you like.

12. Repeat this process for the remaining slides in the project.

13. When finished, preview the project.

14. Once satisfied with the transitions, save and close the project.

Want Some *Drills* for Your New *Skills*?

We have posted labs on our Web site that will enhance and challenge the skills you have learned during lessons presented in this book.

✓ Go to www.iconlogic.com
✓ Click the Learning Center link
✓ Skill it | Drill It | Learn It | Have Fun!

There is no charge to use this service.

Index

A
About IconLogic Books, vii
About the Author, vii
Actions in Real Time, 25
ActionScript 3, 186
Add Effect
    button, 148, 149
Add Text Captions, 31
Adjust background audio
    volume on slides with
    audio, 126
Adobe, 3
Align Mouse to
    Previous/Next Slide, 97
Animation Slides, 146
Appear after, 86, 88
Arrowheads on lines, 94
Artificial voices, 137
Audio
    Advanced Audio, 134
    Free downloads, 124
    Loop, 126
    MP3, 124
    Play button, 124
    Show object level, 134
    Stop audio at end of
        movie, 126
    WAV, 124
Audio split options, 132
Auto calibrate, 129
Auto Capture versus Manual
    Capture, 4
Auto Play, 185
Auto Recording, 23
Automatically use FMR, 198
Autosize Captions, 51

B
Background Audio, 126
Beyond the Essentials
    book, 195
Blank Slide, 75
BMP, 76
Book Conventions, viii

C
Calculate Caption
    Timing, 67
Calibrate a Microphone, 128
Calibrate a recording
    device, 128, 129
Calibrate Input, 129
Callout Type, 65, 92
Callout Type, changing, 111
Camera sounds, 25
Caption Styles, 55
Caption Type, 53
Captions

    Properties, 51
Captions, Insert, 48
Capture interim screen
    shot, 26
Change caption timing, 61
Change Slide Background
    Quality, 74
Click Boxes, 155
    Insert, 155
Collapse to Icons, 11, 13
Constant Bitrate, 128
Constrain proportions, 58
Constrain proportions,
    Images, 78
Continue playing project,
    deselect, 176
Convert Slide Notes to
    Speech, 137
Copy Background, 172
Create an Image
    Watermark, 85
Crop Image, 83
Current Theme Pointers, 96

D
Data Files, download from
    the Web, ix, x
Default Caption Style, 55
Delete a Text Caption, 55
Delete slides, 75
Development Process, 21
    Clean It, 21
    Post It, 21
    Publish It, 21
    Record It, 21
    Rehearse It, 21
    Republish, Repost,
        Retest, 22
    Reset It, 21
    Test It, 22
    Write It, 21
Disable keystroke
    sounds, 25
Display for rest of
    project, 85
Display Resolution, 20, 202
Display Time, Slides, 98
Distribute audio over several
    slides, 132
Drag and Drop actions, 26
Drag and Drop actions,
    capture, 198

E
Edit the Default Caption
    Style, 55, 57
E-Mail, xi
E-mail links, 178

Enable access for assistive
    devices (Mac only), 28
End Point, 93
Export project captions and
    closed captions, 192
Export the Movie's
    Captions, 192
Exporting, 176
Externalize Resources, 185

F
F4V, 140
Fade In Only, 86, 88
Fill & Stroke, 93
Find and Replace, 153
Flash Video, 140, 148
    Change the video's slide
        position, 141
    Force the video to play
        automatically, 143
    Remove the
        playbar, 142
Flashcam, 3
FLV, 140
Fly-In Effect, 148
FMR, 26
FMR Mode, 199
Fraunhofer Institute, 124

G
Generate Captions in
    area, 25
GIF, 144
Go to the next slide action
    (click box), 155

H
Hear camera sounds during
    recording, 25
Hear Keyboard Tap
    Sounds, 25
Highlight Boxes, 104
    Insert, 104
    Reposition, 105
    Resize, 105
Hint captions, 37

I
Image Timing Options, 86
Image Watermarks, 85
Images, 73
    GIF, 76
    JPEG, 76
    Reset to original
        size, 77
    Resize, 77
    Stacks, 88
Import Captions, 194

Increase a slide's Display Time, 98
Input Level OK, 129
Insert a Rollover Slidelet, 118, 120
Insert and Delete Blank Slides, 75
Insert Flash Video, 140
Interface, 7
Item ID, 193

K
Keystrokes, 25

L
Language support, 25
Line Tool, 92
Link a Movie to a Web Site, 176
Links, 176
Links to Web Sites, Creating, 176
Loading screen, 185
Loop audio, 126
Loquendo, 137

M
MAC Executable, 189
Macromedia, 3
Manage Workspace, 14
Manual Recording, 23
Media, Publish as, 189
Menu, creating, 183
Merge an Image into a Slide, 46
Merge an image into a slide's background, 171
Merge into background, 171
Merge with the background, 171
Motion Paths, adding and editing, 149
Mouse click sound, 90
Mouse Click, Showing, 90
Mouse Location And Movement, 31
Mouse Wheel Actions, 26
Mouse Wheel Actions, capture, 198
Move New Windows Inside Recording Area, 26
MP3, 124
MPEG Audio Layer III, 124
Multiple language versions of a movie, creating, 192

N
Narration, 25
Neospeech, 137
New Workspace, 14
Nexus Concepts, 3

Notes, Frame, 127

O
Object Defaults, 48
Object Style Manager, 55, 110, 116, 118, 164
Open Library button, 81
Open Recent Item, 8
Open URL or file, 176
Original Text Caption Data, 193

P
Passive versus Active voice, 153
Paste as Background, 172
Pasteboard, 48
Photo, Add to a TOC (Info), 184
Pick Color, 93
Pick Color tool, 93
Planning New Movies, 4
Play button, 64, 65
Playhead, 64
Pointer Paths, 95, 96
Pointer Type, Change, 97
Pointers, changing and moving, 96
Preloaders, 185
Preview a project, 16
Preview part of a movie, 84
Preview to Next Slide, 105
Preview tool, 16
Print Documents Word Handouts, 190
Project captions and closed captions, Export, 192
Project Information, 182
Project Pointers, 96
Publish files to a folder, 187
Publish to Folder, 187

Q
Question Slides, 164
    % or more of total points to pass, 166
    Add Images, 171
    Allow backward movement, 165
    Allow user to review quiz, 165
    Default Labels, 166
    Graded Question, 168
    Multiple choice, 168
    Pass or Fail, 166
    Quiz Name, 165
    Show Progress, 165
    Show score at end of quiz, 165
    Shuffle Answers, 165

    Specify the correct answer, 170
Question Types, 168
Quizzing Objects, 164

R
Record actions in real time, 25
Record New Project area, 29
Record or create a new project, 29
Recording, 29
Recording Audio, 127
    Microphone placement, 128
    Microphone technique, 128
    Setup, 128
Recording Options, 25, 27, 34, 37, 41
Recording Size, 20
Recording Types, 23
Recording Window, 26
Replace Phrases, 153
Reset Style, 57
Reset Workspace, 12
Resize an image, 77
Resolution and Recording Size, 7
Restore Object Defaults, 48
Retain Text, 160, 161
Reuse a Slide Background, 172
Right-click, 155
RoboDemo, 3
Rollover Captions, 110
Rollover Images, 114
Rollover Slidelets, 118
    Insert, 118
    Stick Slidelet, 119
Round Tripping, 192

S
Screen Resolution, 4
Scripts, 4
Select Unused Items button, 82
Send e-mail to, 178
Shockwave File, 3
Shockwave Flash, 3
Show for rest of slide, 70, 98
Show score at end of quiz, 167
Show/Hide Item, 96
Show/Hide Timeline Objects, 62, 63
Shuffle Answers, 165
Silence, insert, 135
Skins

Apply a Skin, 176
Delete a Skin, 181
Edit and Save a
Skin, 180
Slide, 193
Slide Background
Quality, 74
Slide ID, 193
Slide Quality
High (24-bit), 74
JPEG, 74
Low, 74
Optimized, 74
Speech Agent, 138
Speech Management, 138
Spelling, checker, 67
Split audio across
slides, 132
Standard.js, 189
Start Point, 93
Storyboards, 4
Stroke color, 93
SWF, 3, 144
SWF Conversion, 199
System Tray, 26

T
Task Icon, 26
Text Buttons, 99
Insert, 99
Text Captions
Insert, 48, 51, 54
Resize, 49
Text to Speech, 137
Timeline, 59
Control Caption
Timing, 61
Playback Controls, 59
Playhead, 59
Show, 59
Timeline, hiding, 13
TOC
Create, 183
Project Info, 184
Show, 183
Transition, 86, 88
Transition Effects, 86

U
Updated Text Caption
Data, 193
Use a keyboard shortcut to
go to a slide, 104

V
View Output, 191

W
Want to Learn More?, 195
Watermarks, Creating, 85
WAVE, 124
What is Captivate, 20, 198
Windows Executable, 189
Windows
Executable.exe, 189
Workspace
Manage, 14
New, 14
Workspaces, 9
Applying Skin, 10
Classic, 9
Modify, 11
Navigation, 9
Quizzing, 9
Reset, 11
Widget, 10

Z
ZigZag Effect, 149
Zoom Area, 116
Zoom Destination, 117
Zoom Source, 117

ISBN 1-932733-38-8

53700